ARBITRARY ARRESTS

IN THE SOUTH;

OR,

SCENES

FROM THE

EXPERIENCE OF AN ALABAMA UNIONIST.

BY

R. S. THARIN, A.M.,

A NATIVE OF CHARLESTON, S.C.; FOR THIRTY YEARS A RESI-
DENT OF THE COTTON STATES, AND COMMONLY KNOWN
IN THE WEST AS "THE ALABAMA REFUGEE."

NEGRO UNIVERSITIES PRESS
NEW YORK

Originally published in 1863
by John Bradburn

Reprinted from a copy in the collections
of the Brooklyn Public Library

Reprinted 1969 by
Negro Universities Press
A DIVISION OF GREENWOOD PUBLISHING CORP.
NEW YORK

SBN 8371-2686-X

PRINTED IN UNITED STATES OF AMERICA

TO THE

"POOR WHITE TRASH"

OF THE SOUTH,

AND

"THE MUDSILLS"

OF THE NORTH,

THIS AUTOBIOGRAPHY IS RESPECTFULLY

𝔇𝔢𝔡𝔦𝔠𝔞𝔱𝔢𝔡

BY THEIR FELLOW-CITIZEN AND ADVOCATE,

THE AUTHOR.

CONTENTS.

PREFACE.*

THE hour has at last arrived, when the truth, long trampled under the feet of frenzied mobs, must be heard in the South ; and when the conservative element of the North, long lost sight of and denied, *must* be attended to and *obeyed*.

The time when conservative views (Unionism) have been visited with "punishment" in the South, is passing away; and the time when the same conservative patriotism was brow-beaten in the North, is also passing away.

The liberty of speech, the rights of personal liberty, personal security, and personal property—these *must* hereafter remain intact from the inroads of Radicalism in both sections.

In this great hour of national purification, it is criminal to advocate the perpetuation of selfish feuds. Unless the factious ravings of Radicalism be quelled, the Union cannot be restored. Radicalism *caused* our troubles ; conservatism alone can cure them !

If the cotton-planters calculated on the radical course Abolition has been pursuing,—denying the existence of any Union feeling in the South, and forcing down the throats of truer men than themselves, their own wild doc-

---

* Written before the Proclamation of the President, and before the 22d of September, 1862.

1*

trines *as a test of loyalty,*—if, I say, the courtiers of "King Cotton" based their calculations on such a course in the present administration, and if they acted purposely to produce that very effect, then has their rascality been equaled by their skill and foresight, and we must yield them our admiration as *statesmen,* although we must execrate them as men.

Again, if the advocates of Radical Abolition completely *alienate* the two sections, *in order to preserve the Union,* then *their* statesmanship is worthy of the contempt of all history ; and their hypocrisy will receive its just reward from the hands of an indignant and long-suffering citizen soldiery !

No one denies that slavery is an evil ;

No one denies that adultery is an evil ;

But the Shakers, who advocate absolute non-intercourse between the sexes in order to destroy adultery, are not a whit less ridiculous than those Abolitionists who advocate the utter extermination. or provincial vassalage, of the people of the South in order to destroy *slavery.* They would "make a wilderness, and call it peace."

The personal narrative which follows, embraces the record of that *Unionist* who, although a Southerner by birth, claims the honor of having dealt the *first blow against Secession,* and who narrowly escaped to tell the tale.

While he avoids all allusion to slavery, except incidentally to his narrative, it will, nevertheless, be seen that he considers himself as owing no allegiance to any one institution, North or South, however " peculiar," unless that institution retain its proper dimensions among others.

The reader is invited to the following pages, as a chapter in this strange Rebellion, wherein he may learn how "Southern Rights" were respected in Alabama, in the person of a non-slaveholder of that State,—a native of South Carolina, a graduate of the College of Charleston, S. C., and a former law-partner of William L. Yancey,—whose only offense consisted in his being true to his *oath* to support the Union, and the Constitutions, respectively, of the United States *and of Alabama*.

There are some beings, who, wearing the form of man, consider it the sacred duty of every one to think *with* the crowd who happen to surround him at the time of his utterances. According to this very large class, which has its representatives in every age and clime, sodomy was right until Sodom was destroyed. The only idea they have formed of Lot, is, that public opinion *now* sustains his course, and, *therefore, they* sustain it also. Had they inhabited Sodom, however, in Lot's own time, they would have vociferously condemned the old patriarch as *eccentric*, and would have been as noisy as the other Sodomites in the *mob*, which they would have certainly joined, as a sacred duty to sodomy and Sodom.

There is another class, who would, to-day, justify the mob of Sodom, as having acted to the best of their knowledge and belief.

Another class seize upon an inflamed state of public opinion, to launch upon their neighbors unmitigated evils, on which they fatten and grow great at the public cost.

I may add still another sort of human beings, who, availing themselves of a *status belli*, exasperate the belligerents and the struggle itself, in order to carry a cer-

tain point by its prolongation. Every new element of
vindictiveness and of barbarism, which is added by any
cause,—even by the defeat in battle of their own side,—
they hail as a promise of the success of their own fanatical
notions.

The first class, represented in this unhappy country
by the Secessionists of the South, will have neither the
desire nor the opportunity to listen to reason until mobocracy shall have received a check from the outraged
people of the South.

The second, of which the traitors of the States still
loyal are an example, have the opportunity, but not the
desire, to hear the truth. Because they see around them
much to condemn, they discover in Jeff. Davis every thing
to praise. They offer but an apology for treason.

The third class is to be seen in the perjured leaders of
the Rebellion. They seized upon an inflamed state of
feeling which they themselves had excited, to bring upon
the country a revolution, which *they* are to ride, *they*
hope, into power and greatness. Under the cry of
"Southern Rights," they openly trample upon Southern
Rights.

The other class—the Radicals of the North—seize
upon the belligerent state of the country as a glorious
opportunity for the consummation of their cherished
plans, and, in order to bring about the emancipation of
the slave, deliberately render it almost impossible to
save the Union, or close the war. Under the cry of
"the war for the Union," they fight *against* the Union.*

---

* I beg pardon,—they do not *fight* for any thing. They
"stay at home in order to shape the *policy* of the Nation."—
Vide Fremont's speech at Boston this month (Sept., 1862).
Thus, like the Radicals of the South, who, after precipitat-

But there is another class of men, who, aware of the existence and motives of all the others, will yet pursue the even tenor of their own way, and who, before coming to a conclusion on public or private matters, will weigh the arguments on both sides, and judge for themselves, in accordance with the facts.

I believe this class to be scattered over the length and breadth of this whole nation, both in loyal and disloyal communities, and to them I appeal for a hearing and a just verdict.

To the historian—if he belong to this class—I am not unwilling to leave the rest.

WASHINGTON, D. C., Sept. 11, 1862.

---

ing their poorer neighbors into bloodshed and ruin, are exempt from conscription, if owners of twenty *negroes*, these Radicals of the North, after having deceived hundreds of thousands by the cry, now, alas! no longer true, even in semblance, " the war for the Union," exempt themselves from service in the field, *if stealers of one.*

" Were I the Queen of France, or what's better, Pope of Rome,
  I'd have no fighting men abroad nor weeping maids at
    home ;
  All the world should be at peace, and if fools must show their
    might,
  Why let those who made the battles, be the only ones to
    fight."   *Old Song.*

INTRODUCTION.*

In the month of February, in the year of our Lord 1861, and of *American Independence the 85th*, there appeared in Cincinnati a homeless refugee, whose heart was almost broken, and whose sensitive soul was writhing under wrongs, which his unassisted efforts had been insufficient to obviate or resist.

The victim of that most untamable of all wild beasts, an infuriated and unreasoning mob, he had been exiled from his native South, because the oath he had taken to support the Constitutions *of Alabama* and of the Union, he kept with scrupulous and undisguised devotion to truth and patriotism. The Southern newspapers favorable to Secession, were loud in their hired denunciations. The Charleston *Courier*, a paper which opposed Secession in 1852, denominated him a " renegade" who opposed it in 1861. His offense consisted in undeviating and unadulterated Unionism!

It is to the personal narrative of that political refugee, that the reader's indulgent attention is respectfully invited. It will be advisable to detain the reader, *in limine*, in order to explain matters necessary for the comprehension of the in-

---

* In answer to the question, " Who is he?"

terior and exterior life which is recorded in the ensuing pages.

My first care was to find some one who would recognize me. I was not about to skulk through the world like a whipped cur, but to appeal from my persecutors to the true, the brave, and the conservative all over the country. I was not ashamed, but *proud* of the *cause* of my expatriation ; and I was conscious that misfortune can never overcome entirely a true and loyal heart, unless that misfortune be deserved.

I, therefore, consulted a Directory, proceeded to the "Cincinnati Female Academy," inquired for Professor Milton Sayler (since a prominent member of the Ohio Legislature), who had met me at Richmond, Va., in 1857, at a " Convention of the Young Men's Christian Associations of the United States and British Provinces." By him I was immediately recognized, and introduced, by letter, to Rev. E. G. Robinson, pastor of the 9th-street Baptist Church, and, through him, to the membership generally.

It would be voluminous to mention all the good people who sympathized with me. Levi Coffin, a noble Quaker, afforded the exile an asylum beneath his roof. Col. B. P. Baker, a young, talented, and Christian merchant, now doing business at 62 Front-street, New York, showed me every kindness. Judge Bellamy Storer I was happy to include among my warm personal friends. He indorsed a letter from me to his friend, the President, asking for my appointment as commissioner to Europe, to repel the misstatements of the rebel commissioners, among whom, it will be remembered, was William L. Yancey, my former law-partner, whose antecedent rascalities, and pro-slave-*trade* proclivities, had come under my own observation in Alabama. Judge J. B. Stallo was peculiarly kind and sympathizing. Commissioner Schwartz assisted me in sending for my family, and did all he could to smooth my pathway among strangers.

I soon began to find myself an object of public interest. The newspapers formally announced my presence in the city. I became a subject of constant conversation and comment. I need not say how unsolicited and how unpleasant were the every-day attentions which were becoming fashionable. The Unionists hailed my presence as a proof of the wickedness of Secession. The Abolitionists hailed my advent as a proof of the wickedness of Slavery. I was not a little amused by the persistent suggestions of the latter, who considered me as, *ex necessitate*, one of their number. One of the ladies who resided at " Friend Coffin's," told me I ought to have received " seventy eight lashes, well laid on, to make me an Abolitionist." This lady, who, in other respects, is quite rational, although not national, commences her surname with a " C " and concludes it with an " n." Her first name is Elizabeth.

A Mr. Essex, from Missouri, was also an in-

2

mate. He was a democrat and a gentleman, who sympathized with my sufferings, and will testify to these facts.

I had been able to bring to Cincinnati no documentary proof of the correctness of my statements; and this circumstance began to operate upon the minds of some who had never seen me, and whose politics were never considered particularly obnoxious to Jeff. Davis. Started by these, surmises began to travel through the community as to my *loyalty*, veracity, etc.

These surmises soon became rumors, which became magnified, in timid eyes, to the most ludicrous proportions. Not hearing these things myself, and not supposing such things possible among sensible people, I was somewhat startled to see in the columns of the Cincinnati *Enquirer*, a short editorial, saying I had not told the truth in declaring myself a former partner of Yancey; that I was but a law-student in his office at most, as my youthful appearance would show. These wonderful outgivings of those "pantalooned old women" who began to look upon me as a Secession bomb-shell about to explode in the streets of Cincinnati and deprive them of their modicum of brains, were suddenly brought to a close by the two following extracts, one from the Maysville (Ky.) *Eagle*, the other from the Cahawba (Alabama) *Gazette*.

The following, which I mention *first*, occurred last in point of *time*, but I place it, in substance, here, in order to comment upon the other extract referred to:

"R. S. Tharin, Esq., a former law-partner of William L. Yancey, was mobbed at Collirene, Lowndes county, Alabama, and exiled because he opposed Secession with its own weapons—secret leagues!

"So that is the way you manage down in Dixie! Mr. Yancey may get up a 'secret league' to *destroy* the old Union; but the moment his former law-partner, Mr. Tharin, attempts to counteract his plans by a similar method of procedure, he is barbarously maltreated and unconstitutionally exiled.

"Mr. Tharin is now a political refugee, who, in his own person, is a monument at once of his own daring and of the unsparing villainy of his persecutors."

This needs no comment; it speaks for itself.

It will be proper to state that the Cahawba *Gazette* is, or was, when it could get paper, published in Dallas county, Alabama. The Cincinnati Daily *Press* copied from it the following:

From the Cahawba (Ala.) GAZETTE.

"ORDERED OFF.—We learn from Col. R. Rives,* Collirene, Lowndes county (Alabama), that a man named Robert S. Tharin, a lawyer of Wetumpka (Ala.), was taken up at Collirene last week, tried by a jury of citizens, convicted, punished, and banished from that community for expressing and endeavoring to propagate sentiments that were *dangerous to the peace of society.* He had *conversed* with several *non-*slaveholders in the neighborhood, and proposed to them the organization of a secret Abolition society, and said he was going to establish a newspaper (at Montgomery), to be called the *Non-Slaveholder.* The evidence against him was conclusive. The punishment inflicted was physically slight, although it was degrading."

---

* Pronounced *Reeves.*

There are several features of this short editorial which would repay criticism :

1st. ITS THOROUGH MENDACITY ; that word, " Abolition," the " fruitful source of all our woe," being skillfully interpolated for the basest of purposes. The thing itself, as predicated, was a physical *impossibility*. In the whole cotton region there are not, and never have been (as every Southern man knows), enough Abolitionists to form a " society" of fifty ; nor can any one—not even a sap-headed editorial tool of " King Cotton"—really suppose that I would be *now* living to narrate the events of my miraculous escape, had I been actually convicted of that greatest offense known to the mob in the Sunny South. They would have hanged me without even the *form* of a trial. The publication of the charge was intended to consummate my destruction, because Col. Robert Rives desired to destroy my testimony (which he knew he could only do by destroying my life), and thus to " save his party."

2d. ITS UNBLUSHING EFFRONTERY. *I* " dangerous to the *peace* of society !" Why, look at this Rebellion ! look at its assassinations,* its unparalleled outrages upon American citizens — upon natives of the South ! look at its bloody hands, which would " incarnadine the deep" in the effort

---

* Dr. James Slaughter, to whom was addressed the famous Slaughter (scarlet) Letter by Yancey, soon after his (unauthorized) publication of that " private letter," was found dead in his bed, from the effects of—poison !

to wash them clean! look at its *mobs*—at one time burning (at Montgomery, Alabama) the works of the distinguished Spurgeon ; at another, drunk with blood and blind with fury, sipping out of the skulls of slaughtered soldiers! Yes, look at its mobs, at its pirates, at its utter destitution of moral principle, at its *Radicalism*, and say whether, in my attempt to restrain Alabama from Secession, *I* was dangerous to the *peace* of society!

3d. ITS INSOLENT AND SILLY CHARGES. "He (I) had conversed with several *non*-slaveholders in the neighborhood." "*Conversation*" with "*non*-slaveholders" a crime! *I* consider it a glorious thing to tell the *non*-slaveholders of their wrongs and of their *rights*—"Southern rights!" So far from conversation with *non*-slaveholders being a crime, you will yet learn to your *own* cost, Mr. Editor, that it is conversation (and coalition) with cotton-planters and their editorial dupes, that constitutes the political crime of treason!—another name for which is Radicalism.

"And proposed to them the organization of a secret *Abolition* society!" When Robert Rives inserted that word "Abolition," he thought he did a politic thing. He had told me, after my maltreatment, I "should not escape." He was determined I should *die by another mob*, since he had failed to convince the second that "death was not too severe a punishment ;" and so he thought he would slay me, and save himself by this unfounded charge.

2*

"And said he was going to establish (at Montgomery) a paper, to be called the '*Non-Slaveholder*.'"

"Angels and ministers of grace defend us!" No wonder the planters and the editors trembled in their boots! Indeed! the "poor white trash" have an "*organ!*" "Crucify him! crucify him!!" Why, that's as much as to say that all *white* men were born free and equal!—why, that's returning to first principles with a vengeance!—why, that's —agrarianism! "Crucify him!" What use is there in Calhoun's wonderful and convenient discovery that the Declaration of Independence is a lie and Thomas Jefferson a humbug, if this youngster, Tharin, self-educated, un-cottoned, dares to think, speak, and even *write* for himself and his fellows?

"We are informed," commences the *Gazette*, "by Col. ROBERT RIVES." And *who* is COL. ROBERT RIVES?

Col. Robert Rives was descended from the Huguenots, of whom a portion, as refugees from the barbarous decree of an intolerant Louis of France, selected the banks of the Ashley, in South Carolina, as the place of their exile. Unlike their victim, no blood of 1776 coursed through his veins; but he was a convert to the senseless doctrine of the Charleston *Mercury*, that "*minorities should rule.*"

Rives had been mainly instrumental in raising the mob, voted *against postponing* the publication of the "verdict" until the wife of his victim should be out of danger, and declared that Mr. Tharin should not "escape," *if he could prevent it.*

In spite of the vote of the very mob which he had raised, to suspend the publication of their "proceedings" for four weeks, in order to save the life of an unoffending Southern lady, we find the same Col. Robert Rives sneaking to the office of the Cahawba *Gazette*, a paper not mentioned in the "verdict," and, weeks before the period designated by the mob for its publication elsewhere, procuring, in the very face of his promise to abide by the voice of the meeting, the premature, the murderous advertisement of the very thing he had promised to postpone!

Had the voice of the majority *suited* his ". peculiar" views, Rives would have acted *with* them; but, being in a minority, he got rid of all difficulty on the subject by a very simple process—he seceded!

For such a miserable ignoramus to secede, when his contemptible *minority* had ceased to *rule*, was perfectly natural. Thus, on an exceedingly *small* scale, he illustrated the "principles" of that stupendous crime, which set up the despotic will of a few cotton-planters, and their worse than Helvetic *clienteles*, against the will of the overwhelming majority of the American people, constitutionally expressed.

There is something maddening in the influence

of a mob on a spirit uncontrolled by love of truth. All the passions of the breast, inflamed with fury, then leap up, like fiends above the lava-waves of hell. The eyes roll in liquid insanity; the heart glows with the fires of revenge; the venom of hydrophobia is on the tongue; and, intoxicated by the presence of a concurring mob, deeds of dastardly malignity become the desire and the fruit, which naught save the popularity of the act is quoted to extenuate.

Such a being is no longer a man! he is *lost* to manhood, and to all the qualities which elevate man above the brute creation. Saturated with the poison of his disease, he riots in images of horror and of blood—a Moloch in a Pandemonium of cruel thoughts.

What should be the fate of such a man? What would you do to a dog, mad and foaming, which rushes at the throat of your son?

This Republic owes it to "the Alabama Refugee," and to all her other children who have suffered like him, that the murderous hands which dealt the fiendish blows be no longer uplifted for destruction. In other words, the National and State Governments owe to Unionists, everywhere, protection.

"The wicked shall fall into his own snare." The sneaking behavior of Rives produced the opposite effect from what he designed: *it saved me much inconvenience*, if not danger, by bringing before the attention of the people of Cincinnati a perfect corroboration of the story I myself had told, and *that* from the most unexpected, and, therefore, most reliable source—my very enemies! The charge of Abolitionism no sensible man believed, except the Radicals, from whom it protected me.

The news of the battle of Fort Sumter, 12th April, found Cincinnati wrought up to a degree of excitement unparalleled in the annals of that city. A spontaneous meeting of many thousands collected one night in front of the steps of the Post-office, and various gentlemen addressed the meeting. Some one called my name. The call became general—universal. I rose and commenced thus:

" Fellow-citizens of the United States! I stand before you the representative of the *Union* men of the State of *Alabama*."

This was enough. One spontaneous burst of welcome rose upon the air. Hats were waved; men grasped each other by the hand ; the vast crowd rocked and shouted with an impulse which showed how the heart of Cincinnati bounded with delight at the reception of such intelligence.

The following letter, written by an eye-witness of that scene, will convey the facts better than I could, or would:

" No. 62 FRONT-STREET, NEW YORK, Aug. 11, 1862.

" DEAR SIR : Yours of late date is received, and, but for the fact that I have been slightly indisposed, and a little overworked in consequence of the absence of my partner, B. C., would have had an earlier reply.

" You do right to call me your friend ; for since I heard your earnest and heartfelt plea for the Union before that immense audience at the Post-office at Cincinnati, which chained not only me but hundreds to the spot while you were speaking, I have not ceased to believe you not only loyal and true, but that you deserved something at the hands of Unionists. Your taking a private soldier's place to assist in putting down the Rebellion, shows your pluck and courage. I was glad, while in Washington, to say a word in your behalf, and only wish I could have done more. You ask me to address a letter to the President (in behalf of your appointment as Provisional Governor of Alabama). I regret I cannot render you service in that way, as I do not feel sufficiently acquainted with Mr. Lincoln ; and although I am known to some people in Washington as a Union man, I feel a delicacy in addressing a letter to Mr. Lincoln, even for my friend Tharin.

" As you are at liberty to show this letter, to that intent let me here say, that I believe you to be a true Union man, a real patriot, a Christian, and a man of ability and honor.

" Yours truly,
" B. P. BAKER.

" R. S. THARIN, Esq., Washington, D. C."

The following letter comes in here, as a kind of *post scriptum* to the above:

From HON. CALEB B. SMITH, *Secretary of Interior.*

" DEPARTMENT OF THE INTERIOR,
" Washington, Aug. 25, 1862.

" DEAR SIR :—I am in receipt of your letter of 18th instant, in reference to your appointment as provisional governor of the State of Alabama.

" This is a matter, of course, with which my department has no official connection, and I can only aid you so far as my recommendation may do so.

"I have placed your letter before the President with my recommendation in favor of your appointment, and shall be gratified to learn that your application is successful.

"Yours,

"Very respectfully,

"CALEB B. SMITH,

"*Secretary.*

"R. S. THARIN, Esq."

I have other recommendations for the same place from other sources; but will not insert them here.

I will here state, however, that this application was made while Mr. Lincoln was the unstultified author of the Greeley letter.

From the Sunny South I had brought nothing with me. About three months after my expatriation, however, my wife and two children arrived in Cincinnati. She brought my letter-book, containing, among others, the following letter, in the autograph of Yancey:

"MONTGOMERY, ALABAMA, Oct. 22, 1859.

"DEAR SIR:—I am in receipt of yours of the 20th instant. My business in Coosa county is not large. In fact I have not cultivated it, having, for several years, been expecting to abandon it, to practice in one of the wealthier counties below this. If a legal connection can benefit you in Coosa, I am willing to form one with you, confined to that county. You to receive one-third and I two-thirds of all receipts. If this is agreeable to you, you may consider it as formed, commencing from 1st November next.

"Yours, truly.

"W. L. YANCEY.

"R. S. THARIN, Esq."

Mr. William L. Yancey and his Coosa county partner did not get on very well together, it seems, for the following is an extract from another letter from the former. I have both letters entire in my possession:

"MONTGOMERY, ALABAMA, Dec. 17, 1859.

"* * * * * Be so good, therefore, if you have advertised our connection, to advertise its dissolution. * * * * * *"

I am glad to have it in my power, not only to prove the fact of the partnership, which the Cincinnati *Enquirer* was base enough to *deny* in behalf of its friend Yancey, but also to show that I did not long affiliate, even in *business*, with such a man as Yancey.

But Mr. Yancey is estopped from ever saying a word against me, even in the South, by a "P. S." to the notice of dissolution, in which he "recommended his late law-partner to the confidence of the public, of which he was every way worthy." This appeared in the Hayneville (Lowndes county) *Chronicle*, for the space of a year.

The impossibility of supporting my family in the Queen city of the West, on account of the universal prostration of business, caused me to seek my fortunes in Richmond, Indiana. My friend, James Reeves, wrote me from that city that the opening for a lawyer was good, and I availed myself of the prospect. Before leaving Cincinnati, I deemed it advisable to secure the following letters, which are laid before the reader,

—in the spirit in which this whole chapter is written,—in order to prepare his mind for succeeding chapters, by placing my word, my character, and my experience beyond the possibility of a reasonable doubt :

Letter from Hon. Milton Sayler.

"Cincinnati, Ohio, June 3, 1861.

"It gives me very great pleasure to state that I met the bearer, Robert S. Tharin, Esq., in the annual convention of the Young Men's Christian Associations of the United States and British America, held in the city of Richmond, Va., in May, 1857, to which convention Mr. Tharin was one of three delegates from Charleston, S. C. Mr. Tharin occupied a worthy position in that convention, and, though my acquaintance with him since has been slight, yet I do not hesitate, from my knowledge of him, to commend him to those among whom he may go, as a gentleman in every respect worthy of their good-will and confidence.

"Milton Sayler."

Letter from Samuel Lowry, Esq.

"Cincinnati, June 4, 1861.

"I met the bearer, Mr. R. S. Tharin, at a convention of delegates from the Young Men's Christian Associations of the United States, held at Richmond, Va., May, 1857. He was one of three representatives from the association of Charleston, S. C., had the confidence of his colleagues, and, by his deportment, made a favorable impression on the members of the convention and the citizens of Richmond.

"Samuel Lowry."

Letter from Judge J. B. Stallo.

"Mr. R. S. Tharin, a former law-partner of Mr. Yancey, has been driven from the State of Alabama *on account of his anti-secession sentiments,* and since his expatriation has

3

spent some months in the city of Cincinnati. During his stay here it has been my pleasure to meet him occasionally, and I cheerfully testify that he is a gentleman of culture and of unexceptionable habits, and that he has won the confidence and respect of all who had the good fortune to make his acquaintance.

"J. B. STALLO."

P. S. by REV. E. G. ROBINSON.

"I cheerfully and heartily concur in Judge Stallo's commendation of Mr. Tharin.

"E. G. ROBINSON,
'Pastor 9th-street Baptist Church, Cincinnati."

A Pleasant Reminiscence.

"RESPECTED SIR : By the consent, not only of the teachers and of the committee, but by the request of the pupils of the Hughes High School in general, it was unanimously agreed to tender our heartfelt thanks to you for the eloquent and patriotic oration which you delivered at the unfurling of the Stars and Stripes from the summit of our school.

" With respect,
"J. L. THORNTON,
"J. M. EDWARDS,
"J. T. POMPILLY,
"AMELIA S. WRIGHT,
"MRS. H. B. COONS,
"ELLEN FREEMAN,
"SIDNEY OMOHONDRO, } Committee."
"JOSEPH S. PEEBLES, }

Reply.

"CINCINNATI, OHIO, April 25, 1861.

", LADIES AND GENTLEMEN : I deem it no more than proper to acknowledge, in writing, the receipt of your highly appreciated favor of the 24th instant.

" Your letter of thanks, now before me, will ever be classed among my most cherished mementoes ; and the kindness which dictated it will always retain my affectionate and respectful gratitude.

"In contemplating the many evidences of Cincinnati's Christian hospitality toward myself, I can almost bless the trials which drove me to find a home amid a community so sympathetic and so loyal.

"May our beloved national banner in triumph still wave over *our* city and your school !

"I have the honor, ladies and gentlemen, to subscribe myself, with high regard,

"Your obedient servant,

"R. S. THARIN.

"To the Teachers and Committee
of the Hughes High School."

With my wife and children, now trebly dear to the heart which had lost all other associates save them, I took up the line of my wanderings westward. I bore with me the consciousness of sincerity, and desired nothing so much as *repose*. I longed for some spot of earth where I might support and educate my family, and heal my bleeding wounds with the balm of quiet and study. Richmond, Indiana, generally known as the Quaker City, seemed to invite me to seek needed tranquillity beneath her maples. Alas! how little tranquillity I found there is known to my numerous friends in the State of Indiana.

When I look back upon that period, my soul sickens at the contemplation. Called from my retirement by the voice of the people, at their frequent meetings I would express my views upon the crisis without reserve. My popularity became

greater than I desired, and offensive to those
whose *only* earthly desire *is* popularity.

At length I proposed to the citizens the formation of a " Union Rights Club," at a meeting appointed for the purpose.

The next Saturday there appeared in the "*Broadaxe* of Freedom," which is as much a *Union* paper
as Jeff. Davis is a saint, a ridiculous and menda-
cious criticism of my effort on the night alluded
to. I replied, and the editor acknowledged (in-
advertently) *that he lied.* The next issue of the
Richmond *Palladium* showed the admission of
the *Broadaxe* of its own falsity, and derided the
position of the editor, who had charged me with
being the author of a piece in the *Palladium* (of
the very existence of which I was utterly ignorant)
charging the *Broadaxe* with *Secession* proclivities.

The editor of the *Broadaxe* now perpetrated an
act of which any gentleman would be ashamed.
Instead of acknowledging himself in the wrong,
and retiring gracefully from a controversy, to wage
which decently he showed himself incompetent,
he seized upon the weakest and most vulnerable
point in my fortress.

This was my *Southern origin, my former law-
partnership with Yancey, and my omission to volunteer!*

Pantalooned old women reside in every community. Give them the slightest pabulum for
gossip, and at it they go, as if it was indispensable

to their own happiness to prove every wild surmise of every hair-brained babbler to be true.

The *suggestion* of the *Broadaxe* did its dirty work. At the expense of every principle of honor, the editor of the *Broadaxe* (U. S. Hammond) was victorious. The record of that controversy proves that he *admitted that he lied!* What of that? He was victorious!! At least he, poor fool, so thought, and, doubtless, so thinks to-day.

Driven to the wall by the most unmistakable signs of mobocracy, which, alas! I had learned to detect, I involuntarily volunteered, inviting him to accompany me, which he disgracefully declined.

But *why* should *I*, who suffered so much from Secession, be *driven* to volunteer? Why was I not *already* in the armies of the Union?

I had a *wife*, whom I had promised, when she came, a picture of despair, to Cincinnati with our two small children, that *I would never leave her without her consent.*

For me, *she* had left every relative she had on earth, the sacred dust of her dead, the scenes and companions of her childhood, her brothers impressed into the armies of "King Cotton."

Delicate in health, shattered in constitution, yet heroic and devoted, this young Southern lady, unaccustomed to hardship,—her mother's favorite, most indulged daughter,—was, even then, almost heartbroken at the thought of never seeing again her friends in the South.

She was a stranger in a strange land. She had

3*

no old associations in Richmond, Indiana; she was chilled by the hard, cold, icy manners of the ladies of Richmond, so different from the caressing kindness of Alabama's fair daughters; her little boy was an invalid; her strength was reduced, by our unparalleled sufferings, to the verge of prostration.

Did she not need her husband's presence? Did she not need his guardian care? No mother, no friends, no society,—the wife of an exile, a voluntary exile at his side,—she did need his whole and most devoted society; and it was for the purpose of recuperating her energies, of restoring her health, and of earning a support for her and her children, that I had gone to Richmond.

When she saw the printed demand for the sacrifice, she threw her arms around my neck, and, in a voice broken by sobs, said that she would withhold her consent no longer.

Had she not granted her consent, I would have rotted in Fort Lafayette; I would have suffered myself to be torn into atoms by a Northern mob, headed by an editorial empiric, before I would have broken my word to her. This she knew, and she consented.

Many a regiment would have received me among its field-officers, had I agreed to recruit for it. But my preference fell on the 57th Regiment Indiana Volunteers, the Colonel of which was a native of Virginia, a preacher of the Gospel, and my professed friend!

When I first went to Richmond, I had been introduced to this man by my true friend James Reeves. He, the former, had introduced me to the first audience (at Star Hall) I ever addressed in that city. Elated at my success, he " stuck closer than a brother" to my growing fortunes, was almost every day in my law-office, called at my house and took me to walk almost every Sunday. He would even point me out in church as a persecuted patriot.

What a wonderful instinct has woman! My wife said to me, one day, that she distrusted the sincerity of this clerical gentleman.

I told her that her fears were utterly groundless; and that if the preacher proved false, I would doubt the sincerity of all men.

It is universally known in Richmond that the colonel and lieutenant-colonel of the 57th Regiment both promised me that I should not have to go as a private, on account of my family. The first promised me a field-office anyhow, and the other promised me to use his efforts to obtain for me a lieutenancy, in order that I might be appointed adjutant by the former, if I should desire it.

The lieutenant-colonel handed me a recruiting permit at the People's Bank, authorizing me to recruit a company.

I commenced to address the people of the Fifth Congressional District. The main feature of my speeches was simply "*Union*." I denounced *Eng-*

land as the fomenter of our dismemberment, and prophecied difficulties with that power on the occurrence of the first pretext. This was before the "Trent affair." I always had overflowing audiences, and the good results of my efforts were soon discernible in the communities I visited.

The success of my undertaking was doubtful, however. The emissaries of the *Broadaxe* followed me like my shadow. In private they circulated the hellish invention that I was a "Southern spy." I began to realize the fact that those who had first attacked me were *organized* for my destruction. Probably they felt that as they dared not "go to war" to fight Secessionists, the next best thing they could do would be to destroy the family and prospects of loyal refugees from Rebeldom! The regiment itself became changed toward me. By a few judicious puffs, the *Broadaxe* had completely bought up its vain colonel, who began to turn away at my approach. Poor man! he had promised so many people the same thing, that his rapidly-increasing regiment was in danger of having more officers than privates. *Some* must be thrown overboard! *I* was, of course, a selected victim!

The regiment attained the minimum number; but, although I had labored for that regiment with indefatigable industry (for I desired the pay of an officer for my family made destitute by exile), I was, by the blackest ingratitude, consigned to its ranks.

The following, from the *Palladium* of Dec. 14, 1861, expresses the public feeling of the conservatives* of Richmond :

"Our friend Tharin, failing to raise a company, mainly through the slanders propagated and started by the *Broadaxe* in regard to him, volunteered as a private soldier in the ranks and shouldered his musket,—thus showing his faith in our glorious institutions by his works, and giving the lie to the foul insinuations against him by his persecutor Ham'an. The 57th has no braver man belonging to it than R. S. Tharin ; and we predict that, should the opportunity occur, he will win his way by deeds of valor to promotion, which he already so richly deserves for his exertions in recruiting for this regiment."

From the TRUE REPUBLICAN (*Radical*) *of December* 19, 1861, *published at Centreville, Indiana.*

"R. S. Tharin, Esq., the Alabama refugee, whose name has been so much associated with that of the traitor Yancey, entered McMullen's regiment as a *private*. Mr. T. has resided for several months at Richmond. Failing in an effort to raise a company, he has gone into the ranks. He deserves great credit for his patriotism."

While encamped at Indianapolis I had an interview with the reverend colonel, and demanded that he keep his word, which, it will be remembered, was that I *should not have to go as a private in his regiment.*

After much exciting argument, I forced from him an acknowledgment of his promise, and the next day received a discharge. By-the-by, he himself never went with his regiment.

The following letters explain themselves :

---

* Unionists alone are entitled to this epithet.

From JUDGE JAMES PERRY *to the Colonel of the Sixteenth Regiment, I. V. M., then stationed at Camp Hicks, Md.*

"COL. P. A. HACKLEMAN :*—I beg leave to introduce to your acquaintance, Robert S. Tharin, Esq., a member of the bar, a gentleman of very fair literary and scientific attainments, a native of the South, an emigrant from that land of terror and distress, and loyal to the banner of the Union. Mr. Tharin has rendered valuable services in filling up Col. McMullen's regiment; but, not being very well satisfied with the officers of that regiment, he has by them been permitted to choose another, and has made choice of your regiment, into which he enters as a private soldier. Two motives have directed him to the choice of your regiment : first, the term of service is shorter, and he leaves a family far from any relatives, in a strange land ; secondly, if the country should need his services, after the expiration of the time of enlistment of your regiment, he intends to strive for a better position than that of a private in the service. In his behalf, I ask for such kindness as you have in your power to bestow.

"I am, very sincerely, yours, etc.,

"JAMES PERRY."

From BENJ. W. DAVIS, *Junior Editor of the "Richmond (Ind.) Palladium."*

"RICHMOND, Jan. 12, 1862.

"DEAR SIR :—Permit me, although *personally* a stranger to you, but *otherwise* intimately acquainted with you, to introduce R. S. Tharin, formerly of Alabama, but now of this city, who was driven from that State in consequence of his devotion to the old flag, and who is now a private, a new recruit, in your regiment. It is rumored here that my friend ORAN PERRY is about to be promoted to another regiment in the three years' service, which he well deserves for his sterling good qualities ; and could the appointment of sergeant-major, which he now holds, and which place would be vacant by his transfer, be conferred on my friend R. S. Tharin, either that post, or the

---

* Now General.

adjutancy,—which, I learn, will be vacated for a similar reason, —would be filled by him with equal satisfaction to yourself and regiment *as now*, and it would be rendering a deserved honor to one who is every way worthy and well qualified, beside being appreciated by the numerous friends he has made since sojourning in our little Quaker city.

"Yours truly,

"BENJ. W. DAVIS,

"Jun. Ed. R. *Palladium.*

"COL. P. A. HACKLEMAN."

Let me here mention that the officers and members of the Sixteenth Indiana are deserving of their great popularity and reputation. It was in the tent of the chaplain of the Sixteenth, Rev. Edward Jones, that I wrote the personal narrative which follows. To the gallant and distinguished Col. Hackleman, I owe a brother's love. I have just learned that in the late battle of Corinth, while leading on his *brigade* in the most gallant and heroic manner, the Stars and Stripes waving triumphantly above his head, his gleaming sword encouraging his men, his noble countenance animated with a halo of patriotic zeal, with the word "Forward" upon his lips, he fell into the arms of victory, leaving no stain on his escutcheon, and for his children a heritage of glory.

The following, from the Maryland *Union* (Frederick), is the next link in the chain of the refugee's steps :

"MR. THARIN'S LECTURE.

"FREDERICK, February 10, 1862.

" DEAR SIR :—Understanding, from undoubted authority, that in our very midst is a gentleman, a former law-partner of

William L. Yancey, who has experienced in his own person the extreme of Secession cruelty, and whose love for the Union of his forefathers has been the cause of a martyrdom which history will record as the most remarkable of the nineteenth century, we take the liberty of requesting, in behalf of the patriotic people of Frederick, that you will gratify us by appointing an evening on which to give a narrative of adventures in Alabama, with such remarks in application as you may see fit to deliver.

"We feel warranted in the assurance that the theme will attract an audience second to none which Frederick has produced, and hope you will feel no backwardness in accepting an invitation which is made in good faith.

"In any event, be assured of the sympathy and apprecia-
tion of   "Respectfully,
                              "Your fellow-citizens,
                              "WM. G. COLE
                              "D. J. MARKEY,
                              "CHARLES COLE,
                              "W. MAHONEY,
                              "M. NELSON.
"R. S. THARIN, Esq.

"P. S. With our compliments, will you please invite the field-officers of your regiment (Sixteenth Indiana, we believe) to be present on the occasion?"

"CAMP HICKS, February 11, 1862.

"FELLOW-CITIZENS:—Your flattering and highly-appreciated favor, of yesterday's date, containing an invitation to deliver a lecture on the subject of my adventures and sufferings in behalf of the Union, is just received.

"I hold myself ever ready to address my fellow-citizens of this endangered nation upon the great events which have swept over the Cotton States like a conflagration, consuming as stubble the once sacred rights of American citizens, and threatening to wrap in inextinguishable flames the temple of Liberty. My duty and my inclination alike impel me to expose the horrors of that Reign of Terror which aims at the destruction of republican institutions and the subversion of free speech and free conscience. My own eventful and disastrous experience is the property of the public, who have a right to know just what 'Secession' means.

" Secession aims at the heart of loyalty, whether it pulsates in Northern or Southern breasts. Myself a native of Charleston, S. C., an adopted citizen of Alabama, my wife and children natives of the latter State, my rights were trampled upon the moment I declared my intention to respect the obligation of my oath to support the Constitution of the United States and the Constitution of Alabama. Mobbed, *scourged*, and exiled, I now wander amid a people far from the scenes of my childhood, but not without a feeling of gratitude to that kind Providence who has delivered me from King Cotton, and at the same time afforded me the opportunity of bearing arms in defense of the flag which waved over my ancestral antecedents, which shadowed my cradle with a blessing, and which will receive my corpse when expiring.

" I am happy, therefore, to respond to your kind communication in the affirmative.

" If agreeable to you, I will appoint Saturday evening, the 22d instant, as the time of my lecture—leaving the arrangement of place and hour, etc., to your kind supervision.

" I have the honor, gentlemen, to remain, with highest consideration,   " Your fellow-citizen and servant,

                " R. S. THARIN,

              " Private, 16th Regt. Indiana Vol..

" MR. W. G. COLE and others.

" P. S. The field-officers of the Sixteenth Indiana will be present, if public duties conflict not with their inclinations."

From the MARYLAND UNION.

" AN INTERESTING LECTURE.—It will be seen from the correspondence in to-day's paper, that R. S. Tharin, Esq., former law-partner of Wm. L. Yancey, and at present attached to the Sixteenth Regiment Indiana Volunteers, a gentleman of the highest respectability, of fine accomplishments, endowed with rare talents, and an eloquent speaker, will deliver a lecture in this city on Saturday evening, the 22d instant. Due notice of the hour and place of meeting will be given, and we hope there will be a general outpouring on the part of our citizens to hear him, as we feel assured that the lecture will be unusually interesting, and delivered in the finest style."

One of the aids to Gen. Banks about this time detailed me from my regiment to write for him at headquarters, where I remained until some time after the battle of Winchester.

The lecture was never delivered. The division of Gen. Banks was ordered to march into Virginia. I went with my regiment, of course. The following certificate will explain what I was about in Virginia:

Certificate from CAPT. M. C. WELSH, I. V. M.

"WOODSTOCK, VA., April 2, 1862.

"I take pleasure in stating that R. S. Tharin, Esq., of the 16th Indiana, although exempt from such duty at the time, as clerk on Gen. Banks' staff, to my certain knowledge borrowed a gun and accouterments from one of my men (Evans Armstrong), and did his devoir at the great battle of Winchester, on Sunday, 23d March, 1862.

"M. C. WELSH,
"*Capt. of Comp. D, 7th Ind. Vols.*"

Having finished my duties at headquarters, I was proceeding, *via* Washington, to rejoin my regiment, when I was detained in this city (Washington) by the reception of a small office in the Treasury Department. My regiment's term of service in a few days afterward expired. I received my discharge and my pay, and proceeded to Indiana for my family, who are now, thank God, once more with their natural protector.

I will conclude this introductory chapter with a letter to the London *Daily News*, to a careful perusal of which the reader is invited, as it proves the pro-slave-trade proclivities of William L. Yancey, *then commissioner in London* of the Confederate States, so called. It appeared in the columns (4th and 5th) of the London *Daily News* of November 27, 1861 (page 2).

"YANCEY AND THE SLAVE-TRADE.

CONNERSVILLE, INDIANA, October, 1861.

" *To the Editor of the 'Daily News.'*

"SIR: In a recent issue of the *Times* I see a letter from 'Hon.' William L. Yancey, one of the commissioners of the pasteboard 'Confederacy,' of which he is chief architect, in which epistle he attempts to show that, in the Southern Commercial Convention at Montgomery, State of Alabama, in May, 1858, he was not in favor of the renewal of the African slave-trade.

"To that Convention—which has identified itself with the most obnoxious measures ever resorted to for the violation of the time-honored principles and reciprocal stipulations of both Great Britain and America—it was my good, or bad, fortune to be a delegate.

"Interested as, in spite of my indignation, I felt myself in the great debate, that for five consecutive days occupied the exclusive attention of the body, I followed up the argument in all its sickening details, watched every parliamentary and unparliamentary shift to keep it exclusively before the convention, and, although disgusted by the sophistries used by all the parties to the discussion, watched its inception, progress, and conclusion as I would have watched a gathering avalanche upon a mountain-top.

"The eloquent champion of the slave-trade on that memorable occasion was William L. Yancey! In fluent periods he poured out the cataract of his oratory in favor of a measure which, if successful, could prove no less than the revival of the accursed traffic in human flesh.

"Leonidas Spratt, of South Carolina, whose whole notoriety and Southern popularity are derived from his slave-trade monomania, and who has since published in Mr. Yancey's 'organ,' the Montgomery *Advertiser*, his prediction of 'another revolution,' on account of the temporary prohibition (by the Provisional Congress) of his darling measure, had, at the previous session of the Southern Commercial Convention (1857), introduced a resolution expressly demanding its revival. Of a committee appointed to report, at the next session, 'on the advisability of reopening the African slave-trade,' Mr. Spratt, by virtue of his motion, was constituted chairman, and Mr. Yancey enjoyed the honor of being named second on that humane committee.

"The year's recess having expired, we find, at Montgomery, in 1858, Yancey, Spratt, and the 'Southern Commercial Convention.' Mr. Spratt introduced a long, elaborate, and incomprehensible report, abounding in scientific terms, and propounding a new governmental and social theory, which to nine-tenths of the assembly was like the handwriting on the wall, in need of an interpreter. When, to the great relief of the unscientific ear of the 'Southern Commercial Convention,' Mr. Spratt had concluded his long-spun production, Mr. Yancey arose and said, substantially, that

"'Although he agreed with every word of his amiable and patriotic friend, Mr. Spratt, still he considered the magnificent report of that gentleman too unwieldy for parliamentary purposes, and that, therefore, as a minority report, which he would move as a substitute to the original, he would offer the following resolution :

"'*Resolved*, That the Federal laws repealing the African slave-trade ought to be repealed.'

"Mr. Yancey was too good a lawyer to be ignorant of the full force and meaning of the legal term 'repealed,' which was enunciated with significant and sonorous emphasis. Whether, at its inception, the slave-trade was customary or statutory, the 'repeal' of the 'statute' prohibiting its continuance is susceptible of but one meaning, and that—its resumption. In effect, Mr. Yancey's resolution, without the least change in its meaning, might have been worded :

" ' *Resolved*, That the African slave-trade ought to be revived.'

"In fact, the debate which ensued on the introduction of the Yancey substitute, and which consumed about five days, to the exclusion of all other matter, was conducted altogether upon the supposition that the resolution contemplated the revival of the trade. With this universal opinion the convention listened to the arguments *pro* and *con.* Upon the square issue of renewal, or non-renewal, each debater took his ground. The most prominent of these were Roger A. Pryor, editor of the Richmond *South*, published in Virginia, and William L. Yancey, of Alabama.

"Mr. Pryor opposed Mr. Yancey on several grounds, one of which I remember to have been that the 'minimum of labor produces the maximum of value,' which Mr. Yancey combated with great enthusiasm. He showed that the 'minimum of labor' would benefit Virginia, who raises the laborers, but would injure the cotton States, which consumes them. He ridiculed Virginia for her want of Southern sentiment, and foretold her dismemberment, if not her entire defection to 'Abolitiondom,' as he was pleased to call the public opinion of Christendom.

" 'No!' substantially exclaimed the advocate of piracy, 'No! I hope the hour is not far distant, when the cotton States, no longer dependent on the slave-producers of Virginia, will scatter among their people a wealth of negroes, which will enable every white man to own one or more. At the present ruinous prices, which accrue to the benefit of Virginia and Kentucky only, there is danger of such a reduction in the number of owners that there might be a collision between the slaveholders and non-slaveholders, which would dethrone King Cotton and destroy his influence forever; and that the only way to avert this impending crisis, was to import, from Africa, cheap laborers for the benefit of the cotton-growing States.

4*

He said that Virginia was incapable of supplying the increas-
ing demand at any price, and that, even if she could, the result
must be fatal, for that the Africans were rapidly losing their
color and other valuable qualities in the great Caucasian race,
and needed a fresh infusion of pure African blood to prevent
their entire absorption.'

"It is not my intention to give a synopsis of the fiery denunciations that constituted the staple of Mr. Yancey's speeches
in that assembly. Suffice it to say, that, while in his whole
tirade, he did not once, even by implication, disclaim his desire to reopen the African slave-trade, he denounced the Federal
laws prohibiting it, as partial to the Northern manufacturers,
and hostile, in spirit, to the agricultural and commercial interests of the cotton-growing States. He did not hesitate to
denounce Wilberforce as a whimsical sentimentalist, and even
pronounced England herself a pseudo-philanthropist, who, if
ever she dared to interfere against King Cotton, would find
herself reduced, before the eyes of the world, to the melancholy
alternative of domestic misery and revolt, or of confining her
charities to her own suffering subjects at home.

"Here let me parenthesise, that whenever such men as William L. Yancey speak of the South, they never mean the non-
slaveholders, who represent the numerical proportion of fifteen to one as compared with the ' planters,' or slaveholders.

"Although, in this republican form of government, which
claims the people as the sovereign, and a majority as the
ruler, the non-slaveholders are, by far, the most important
class, yet, on account of the skillful agitation of the slavery
question, the slaveholders have obtained a despotic mastery,
and allude exclusively to themselves and *their* property, when
they use the expressions 'the South,' ' Southern interests,' &c.

"In order to ' defend the South' and ' her institutions,' from
the encroachments of the public opinion of Christendom, and
the uncomfortable juxtaposition of light with darkness, secret
leagues and associations were inaugurated, consisting entirely
of sworn conspirators, who, being silently armed with the
stolen guns of the unsuspecting government, resisted the laws
by seizing the forts, arsenals, and property of that government,
to the great astonishment of the uninitiated of both the South

and the North. Thus, possessing all the implements of military power, this diabolical mob stifled every breath of remonstrance, and almost every thought of resistance. Some of the oppressed and insulted Unionists (myself among the number) openly opposed the reign of terror, which was studiously produced by Yancey and his colleagues. False imprisonments, murders, expatriation, 'cruel and unusual punishments,'—the torture by cowhide, tar and feathers, and fence-rails, public and private confiscations,—these were the coercives which ensued, and which immolated, on the very altars whereon these men had sought to sacrifice their country, the freedom of the press and the liberty of speech.

" The writer of this, formerly the partner in law of Yancey, but true to his oath to support the Constitution and the Union, was mobbed in Alabama, not far from Montgomery, because he determined to lose his life, before he would consent to gain it by submitting to such an unholy usurpation. Frequently approached on the subject of identifying himself with the secret league of United Southerners (the offspring of Yancey's perfidy and genius), he persistently refused ; frequently 'cried down' at public meetings, when he but endeavored to fulfill his obligations to his non-slaveholding brethren, he would try it again, until he was finally mobbed, maltreated, and exiled ' by some of the most respectable citizens' of Lowndes county, contrary to the laws of the United States, of the Confederate States, and contrary to the unrepealed statute of the State of Alabama.

" But, although ill-used, he still survives, and, from that unmerited obscurity to which his enemies have endeavored to consign him, he keeps a bright lookout upon the game which his country's (and his own) enemies are playing, and now and then defeats the intentions of corrupt players when they endeavor to cheat.

" If I can advance the cause of truth, justice, and our still glorious, because righteous, Union, I will be better pleased with my humble fate, than to enjoy all the hospitalities of a gorgeous court by a system of intrigue and falsehood unparalleled in history. No true gentleman considers me 'degraded' by what has been done by a brutal mob, and, despite my misfortunes, I remain infinitely above my late partner in law, because I have ever refused to become his partner in crime!

"Independently of the patriotism which impels me to cherish the Union of my fathers, I am really solicitous that Great Britain, the land of my ancestry on both sides of the house, shall not ignore all her grand legislation on this subject, and lend her powerful aid to reinstate the foulest traffic known to history.

"Of my British descent I am justly proud. Col. William Cunnington, whose relations of that name still live (in London, I believe), was the lineal maternal ancestor of my father. In the time of nullification in South Carolina (1832), my father was the only Unionist out of four brothers. I have the proud satisfaction of being true, therefore, not only to my country and my oath, but also to the memory of him, whose sacred dust I am interdicted by the fiends of mobocracy from revisiting.

"I am not permitted to correspond with the mother from whose presence I was illegally and cruelly torn. I know not whether she be still alive. If she be, may these tearful lines convey to her the assurance, so necessary to a mother's heart, that her ill-used son (with his expatriated family) is alive and well.

> " 'Oh! if there be, in this world of care,
> A boon, an offering, Heaven holds dear,
> 'Tis the last libation Liberty draws
> From the heart that bleeds and breaks in her cause!'

"This reflection is my rich reward and my consolation.
"I am, &c.,
"ROBERT S. THARIN."

The following, from the Richmond (Indiana) *Palladium* of January 4, 1862, edited by the Hon. D. P. Holloway, and the high-souled, patriotic, and talented Ben. Davis, is, not inappropriately, added here:

"THARIN vs. YANCEY.

"Some time ago, R. S. Tharin, Esq., of this city, informed us he had written to the London *News*, refuting the position taken by Yancey in the London *Times*, that he (Yancey) was not nor ever had been in favor of reopening the African slave-trade. We notice in the Cincinnati Daily *Commercial* of Dec. 21, the following allusion to that letter. The *Commercial* locates our friend Tharin as being in London at the time of his writing the letter, which is a mistake, as he was at Connersville on a recruiting expedition for the 57th Regiment, at the time he penned the article. The *Commercial* says:

" 'In a recent letter to the London *Times*, Mr. William L. Yancey, one of the so-called commissioners from Jeff. Davis's bogus government, tried to conciliate our English brethren by asserting that he had never been in favor of the renewal of the African slave-trade. Unfortunately for Yancey, this intrepid falsehood fell under the notice of his old law-partner, Mr. Robert S. Tharin, in London at the time, and who, in a letter to the *News*, shows that Yancey is as big a liar as he is a traitor. Both Mr. Yancey and Mr. Tharin were delegates to the Southern Commercial Convention at Montgomery, May, 1858; and, at that convention, Yancey "denounced the Federal laws prohibiting the slave-trade, as partial to the Northern manufacturer, and hostile in spirit to the agricultural and commercial interests of the cotton-growing States." He, at the same time, offered the following resolution:

" '*Resolved*, That the Federal laws prohibiting the African slave-trade ought to be repealed.

" 'This disposes of Yancey's claim to veracity, and shows how worthy a representative he is of that prince of liars and repudiators, Jeff. Davis.' "

Before proceeding with my adventures and sufferings in Alabama, I will here premise, that this chapter was written merely for the purpose of preparing the reader for what is to follow, by placing before him such Northern and Southern testimony as will give me a title to his attention in the ensuing pages.

For all real or apparent egotism in this and in the ensuing chapters, I must apologize on the very threshold. I know how difficult it would be to avoid egotism in an autobiography. The very undertaking is an egotism. But, from my adventures, *if any legal fact or any other truth be retrieved from oblivion*, I shall not regret the risk to which I subject myself in entering, at this time, the field of literature.

I hope I am writing more for the good of my country than for my own. Of this the reader must form his own judgment from the moderation, or the contrary, of my style, and my manner of treating facts.

It will be necessary, of course, to give some preliminary remarks at the outset, explaining my presence in Alabama, my antecedents, and some few occurrences immediately preceding the outrages upon *my* Southern Rights, which it is the duty of this work to record.

SCENE THE FIRST.

MY OATH.

"I do solemnly swear to support the Constitution of the
United States and the Constitution of Alabama; and never,
for considerations personal to myself, to neglect the cause of
the defenseless and oppressed."

Oath of admission to the Alabama Bar.

FOR this hour I have waited with all the patience of one who always knew that it must come
—who always anticipated the present glorious
attitude of the Democratic party.

Radicalism must, of necessity, fail to administer
the government of a nation so extensive and so
free as ours. The Union is at once the cause and
the effect of Conservatism. It was to be expected
that the inception of hostilities, by action and reaction, would bring about sectional antagonisms.
This was the aim and the hope of the diabolical
clique who "precipitated the Cotton States into a
revolution." Unionism in the South was "tarred
and feathered;" Unionism in the North was denounced as "proslavery." Yancey in the South,
Greeley in the North, belong, in fact, to the same
party—Disunion!

But it was also to be expected that the unnatural excitement would wear off, and common

sense reinstate itself, when mobocracy and Lynch law would disgust even their own advocates.

Freedom of speech and of the press will be the outgrowth of the very oppressions which have muzzled the expression of conservative Unionism in the South and in the North. The very *names* of "North" and "South" will perish from the memory, and the malignity of sectionalism will die for the want of a basis of operations.

If this book, baptized in the blood and charred by the fires of a revolution, the occurrence of which I periled my life to prevent, shall add one atom of success, one drop of power, to that great Niagara of Conservative Unionism which is soon to burst over both sections in irresistible force—washing out the blood-stains of Radicalism, together with the unpatriotic names of "North" and "South,"—it will, just so far, accomplish the principal purpose for which it is now dedicated to my whole—my bleeding country.

I was born on the paternal estate of "Magnolia," just outside of the corporate limits of the city of Charleston, S. C., on the 10th day of January, 1830. After many hardships, I obtained, by my own perseverance, from the College of Charleston, my degree of A. B. in March, 1857; and in the State of Alabama, to which I had emigrated in September, 1857, I received my degree of A. M. in 1860.

My ancestry, on both sides of the house, were decent people. I am not ashamed to record that

William Cunnington, my lineal paternal ancestor, was a revolutionary colonel, under Gen. Francis Marion, the great "Swamp Fox" of Carolina history. Nor will it bring the blush of shame to my cheek to say that my maternal grandfather, the Rev. Robert S. Symmes, was a graduate of Queen's College, Oxford, in England, of which realm he was a native, and that he held a high place among the literati of the Queen city of the South. My honored father—may he rest in peace!—needs no higher eulogy than that, in 1832, he was the only Unionist of four brothers; and that, in 1852, and even up to the time of his decease, he remained firmly devoted to the integrity of the nation!

My uncle Theodore, a Co-operationist in 1852, a Secessionist in 1862, rejoices in the possession of the life-size likeness of Col. Wm. Cunnington, his *Union* grandfather!

My uncle Edward keeps, as an heir-loom, the likeness of the Father of his country, presented by his own sacred hand to my grandmother under the following inspiring circumstances:

Under the magnificent "magnolia," from which the whole Cunnington estate was called—and under whose mighty branches my early boyhood was mostly passed—was grouped a dinner party, in honor of a visit from Gen. George Washington to his intimate friend Col. Cunnington. The toasts were over, the company were about to rise, when a lovely apparition riveted all eyes to the table.

Arrayed in a dress, composed of the stars and

5

stripes, stood a little girl, with a full-blown magnolia (or "laurel," as it is commonly called there)
in her right hand. With childish simplicity she
approached the great Washington—who was accustomed to such tributes, and who was not at
all abashed, although a very modest man, by so
pointed an action—and lisped these words:

" Will General Washington, who has won so
many unfading laurels already, accept of this emblem of his greatness from a very little girl ?"

Amid the smiles of the company, the Father of
his country, taking the gift, rose, and, being a
man of but few words, took from his finger a ring,
containing a likeness of himself (which I have
often seen), and handed it to my grandmother,
whom he at the same time affectionately kissed.

Could General Washington rise from his grave,
he would see most of the descendants of that little
girl, who has long since left this world of trouble,
struggling to overthrow that Union for which he
spilled his blood, and the perpetuation of which
he strenuously and repeatedly urged upon them
in his prophetic Farewell Address!

Could Col. Cunnington revisit the scenes of his
usefulness, he would request that the name of
"Cunnington" be dropped from the names of
those of his descendants who have disgraced it
by disunionism, retained by my deceased Union
father, and *added* to the name of him who writes
these filial words.

My immigration to Alabama was not the result

of a preference for that State. I was invited thither by letter. William B. Peurifoy, an old school and college friend and classmate, wrote me that my presence in Wetumpka was solicited as a teacher of the male academy at that place. I went in consequence of that letter, and found the city of Wetumpka, like Washington, a " city of magnificent distances." The buildings, however, were neither so large nor so numerous as those of the latter city. From the refined " Queen city of the South" to the rural town of Wetumpka was a letting down; but I determined to do my duty to the children under my charge, and I did it.

In the spring term of 1859, I was admitted to the practice of law at Rockford, Coosa county, Alabama. Judge Porter King, now a Secessionist, and *always* a Disunionist, administered the oath, which I signed in open court, and by which I solemnly swore (as every admitted lawyer in the room, including the judge himself and Wm. L. Yancey, had done) " *to support the Constitution of the United States and the Constitution of Alabama, and never, for considerations personal to myself, to neglect the cause of the defenseless and the oppressed.*" As this narrative is developed, the reader will become convinced that it was for making myself an exception to the members of the bar, and the national and State officials, *by religiously and firmly keeping my oath*, that I suffered the horrors of persecution in the reign of terror so soon to ensue.

No sooner had I opened my law-office in Wetumpka, than an opportunity occurred for me to
risk something for the sake of my oath.   One of
the "poor white trash" was dragged down to the
margin of the river, laid across a log, and whipped
by a throng of blackguards, on the charge that he
sold liquor to negroes.   They had charged him
once with being a negro, and, afterwards, with
associating with negroes.   He was ridden on a
rail until his clothes were literally torn off his
body.   From the lintel of his own door he was
repeatedly hanged until he was black in the face.
This victim of unauthorized power sought my
office and asked my advice.   He was a pitiable
object.   Fright and general bad usage had left
their marks upon him.   I could not refrain from
smiling, as he entered in palpable alarm, lest I
should kick him down stairs for asking for his
rights.   My eyes were not quite closed to the
condition of the South even then (1859).   I had
felt some very unpleasant and some very indignant emotions, when seeing the prostration of the
many at the footstool of the few.

Franklin Veitch, as he called himself, commenced his story.   During its recital, sometimes
he would stand on one foot, sometimes on the
other, his hat traveling about from one hand to
the other, from his head to the chair, from the
chair to his head.   He sat down at my invitation,
but, the seat of his pants having been ridden off
on the jagged fence-rail the night before, the cold

contact of the chair started him back to his feet;
and I involuntarily burst into loud laughter. My
mirth was echoed from the pavement beneath my
window.

Poor Veitch was overwhelmed. Seizing his
hat, and turning upon me a reproachful glance,
which conveyed a lugubrious " *et tu, Brute,*" expression, he muttered in a tone which cut me to
the heart, " *There ain't no justice in Alabama!*"

I felt humiliated. I approached the poor trembling victim of mobocracy. I looked with changed
feelings upon him. Encouraged by my manner,
he raised his cowering eyes. Fear had added a
gleam of almost insanity to their expression; but
there was a ray of hopeful intelligence, as he
caught my pitying glance, which was very touching.

" Mr. Veitch, who sent you to me?"

" Mr. Hill."

" What do you want?"

" Fair play."

" Do you want my services as a lawyer?"

" Yes, sir."

" You are too much excited now—come to me
next week."

"Will you take my case *then?*"

"May be so."

Veitch retired.

Having made inquiry as to the facts of the
case, I found that Veitch had been a victim to
even worse than that of which he complained.

My oath, "*never, for considerations personal to myself, to neglect the cause of the defenseless and oppressed,*" returned to my recollection. I found that to keep that oath would subject me to great loss of popularity, because the ringleaders of the little mob were the most popular of the young men of the town, long residents, and endowed with negro property, that great passport to impunity.

In order to show the reader the fatal alternative which was presenting itself before my mind, I will explain to him that I was not myself a slaveholder, and that I was ambitious of success in the noble profession of my choice, for which I have always had a passion.

I almost hoped that Veitch would *not* come back. As the time drew near I thought he had forgotten; but no! he came, and again asked me to take his case. He even *urged* me to take it for the sake of *justice.*

I did not believe him to be a *worthy* man. I thought him a low-minded wretch, as he afterward proved; but I *knew* him to be "defenseless and oppressed."

This was an unpleasant predicament. I felt a strange anger against Veitch; I almost hated him for being "defenseless" and for being "oppressed."

But I took his case. Thank God, *I kept my oath!* How few lawyers, alas! can say that they kept their oaths when interest opposed duty!

Then dawned DAY THE FIRST of my bitter but

virtuous experience—a struggle that shook the whole community. The parties sued became more than ever unmerciful to Veitch. They threatened to kill him, if he did not leave the commuuity in so many hours; they offered him bribes. The poor whites of the town secretly encouraged him to remain. The case was docketed, and the time of court was approaching. What the defendants had to do must be done quickly. Veitch disappeared. I appeared at court; the case was called, and a paper was produced by the defendants dismissing the case, and signed "Franklin $\overset{His}{\times}$ Veitch." $\underset{mark.}{}$ I offered to prove duress; but the judge dismissed the matter with indecent haste.

This *non*-slaveholder had yielded his rights through *fear*, and had allowed himself to be taken out of the town.* I have never heard *from* him since, but it seemed to me, at one time, I would never cease to hear *of* him. I became the most unpopular man in Wetumpka. Lies had been freely circulated pending the trial. *For keeping my oath in that case, I almost lost all.* But there were other counties in which I practiced with immediate success.

Franklin Veitch was sent into my office by a divine power, in order that I might receive my sight. Before that circumstance, I had seen events dimly, and "men, like trees walking;" but, with

---

* To Columbus, Georgia, I believe.

a sudden unpleasant awakening, I found myself
in a modern Sodom, and felt my blood curdle
within me at the recollection that the class to
which Veitch belonged had been growing more
and more degraded, more "defenseless" and more
"oppressed," ever since I could remember.

In my native South Carolina I had been too
young to note the workings of aristocracy upon
the oppressed poor. Every one in that State is
too busy in the praiseworthy task of identifying
him or herself with the "powers that be,"—in
tracing their "respectability" to the fountain-head
of the first families, whether whig or tory, and in
finding out some unfortunate family upon whom
to look down,—too much absorbed in such de-
lightful and ennobling pursuits to pause for the
scrutinizing of the flaws in the "system of civilization" in which, as primaries or satellites, they
all unconsciously revolve. Reared in the midst
of aristocratic pretension, my youthful days were
stained with a pride of which I am now heartily
ashamed, and the utter meanness of which it has
been given me to discover and renounce. I pity,
from my soul, the bigoted vacuity of the man who,
in the hard-handed mechanic, upon whose perspi-
ration he lives, as the fly lives in the exhalations
of the horse or the ox, can see only society's
"mudsill," and in himself discovers the superstructure, which *debases* the system upon which
it rests. But I was gradually drawn to this
higher stand-point. I ascended the slope of dis-

covery with painful steps. The sensible horizon
is ever in the way of the rational horizon. I had,
as it were, to mount above and beyond the petty
elevation of education, and, by actual insight, by
ocular revelation, coupled with the sublime influence of a recorded and a solemn oath, to meet the
usurper face to face, before I could discover the
cause of so much woe, the origin of so much evil
as was constantly passing before my eyes.

There are many Franklin Veitches in the South
to-day—many in the army of Secession ; and for
every Franklin Veitch there is a perjured lawyer ;
and for every perjured lawyer, an outraged State
Constitution. The leaders of the conspiracy are
loud in their exclamations for *State rights;* but
their whole scheme is based upon the destruction
of State and personal rights. They pretend to
Southern independence, but ignore the personal
independence of the white people of the South ;
they shout " Southern rights," yet they have completely *annihilated Southern rights: mine,* alas!
are—where ?

The Secessionists have trampled upon the Constitution of the United States, the bills of rights of
the several Southern States, and the "Constitution
of the Confederate States of America"—every
provision of each of which relating to personal
security they have, from first to last, deliberately
ignored.

This occurred in 1859. Thus early my mind
was, unhappily for myself and family—but for

some good purpose I must think—set to work upon the subject of "*Southern Rights.*"

There was *another* cause, which placed me in an unpopular attitude in Alabama. I had advocated, in a series of articles, in the Wetumpka *Enquirer*, the establishment of *small farms*, and the use of the water-power of the falls and rapids of the Coosa, which flows through that village. I had proved the injurious effects upon the "*the people*" of over-grown plantations, and had expressed the belief that Wetumpka would soon eclipse Montgomery, should a judicious application be made of the water-power and the mineral, medicinal, and agricültural elements of success which abounded all around and within her. I also advocated the abolition of all monopolies: such as the penitentiary system, by which the crime of the State was engaged in industrial pursuits, to the loss of the virtuous poor mechanic. I was never popular with the cotton-planters after that. Small farms would benefit the "masses," and *that* would injure *them;* agricultural pursuits would make white men *see* their interests, and that would diminish the power of "King Cotton." But greater events soon occupied the attention of all minds.

It was some time before the occurrence just recorded, that the infamous John Brown raid occurred. I make no apologies for my own course at that time, which was to offer a series of resolutions, at a large public meeting at Wetumpka, strongly

condemnatory of such diabolical outlawry, and
demanding the protection of the Federal power to
preserve the States from invasion. These resolutions were unanimously adopted. The resolutions
were published in the Montgomery *Advertiser* of
that period.

I had been led to suppose the John Brown raid
to be the first of a series. I had not yet heard
the truth—nor was it until long afterward that I
perused the declaration of John Minor Botts, in
his appeal to the people of Virginia, that the governor of Virginia admitted that he knew it to be
a farce, and only seized upon it to stir the blood
of Virginia to the notes of war.

I must not omit to mention that, at that meeting, *contrary to my express desire*, a vigilance
committee was appointed, that I was included in
that committee, and that, at their first meeting,
which was in my office, I proposed to them the
resolving ourselves into a nucleus for a new *national party*, to be called the *Union party*. I presented them a paper, for their signatures. The
proposition was met with indignation, and my
name was, at my desire, dropped from the membership of the committee.

I then appealed to the citizens of Wetumpka
personally. A few only responded—each saying
he wanted the Union, but the democratic party
would save it. (This was *before* the "split" in
Charleston, S. C.) I remember Col. Saxon especially said it was a good thing, but that the Na-

tional Democracy would yet save the Union—a
prophecy which will, I think, be soon fulfilled.

About this time, at Montgomery, fourteen miles
off, an advertisement appeared calling upon the
citizens to meet for the formation of a "LEAGUE
OF UNITED SOUTHERNERS." A great deal of excitement was the consequence, and so it was
announced, a short time afterward, that it had
failed. But it had *not* failed. It was formed
into a *secret* league, although I, among others,
supposed at the time it had failed. *I believe it
exists to-day.* Yancey was and *is* the chief.

The State of Alabama, after the call for a
League, became alive with transparencies. Every
town was full of "Knights of Malta." Wetumpka had its secret order of Knights, who carried
about their transparencies illuminated with sym-
bolic characters. "R., 1861" was conspicuous
on them. I was asked if I would join them. I
demanded to know their objects. The objects
were *secret*, but for the benefit of the "South."
In what way? Joining was the only way to
know.

I did *not* join. I was at my home each night
at early candlelight, and never left till morning;
but *I, too*, was working for the good of the *true*
South. I was studying the census of 1850, and
preparing myself to tell the people truths which
they never had been permitted to know before.

But I must not anticipate.

My politics were national democratic. I was

for the nomination of Stephen A. Douglas, *as the only candidate who could save the Union by his election.* When the "great split" occurred at Charleston, I was completely undecided what to do. I was disposed then to condemn the persistency of the Douglas wing in keeping their nominee before the convention, when they must have seen the danger of disruption which such a course involved. Not to detain the reader, however, on mere questions of expediency, suffice it to say that, after deep reflection upon the duties of every American citizen in such a crisis, I resolved to select those candidates who were most unequivocally for the " *Union*, the Constitution, and the enforcement of the Laws." This I did without any sacrifice of my *national* democracy.

During the great presidential canvass, which resulted in the lamentable elevation of Abraham Lincoln to the chief magistracy, I was frequent in my addresses to the people on the one inexhaustible theme of the Union and the Constitution.

As an elector for the Bell-Everett ticket, my favorite argument in support of my position was the Farewell Address of that greatest of Southerners, George Washington. While I obtained the plaudits of my own party, I became the object of mingled fear and hatred by the disunion demagogues of my adopted State. Disgraceful scenes would often occur, when, warmed with my noble theme, I would launch a fiery denunciation at the head of Yancey, with whom my law-partnership

6

had been some time at an end. Several times I was openly threatened with "tar and feathers," and once was hooted down from the rostrum.

It was during the heat of the presidential campaign, that the Hon. Jabez L. M. Curry, member of Congress for the 7th Congressional District of Alabama, advertised himself to speak at the town of Wetumpka. Haggerty Hall was crowded with a dense mass of people of all parties to hear the Congressman on the exciting questions of the day. During the progress of his remarks, the orator exclaimed :

"As soon as Abe Lincoln takes the Presidential chair, five hundred thousand Wide-awakes, already drilling for the purpose, will rush over the border, lay waste your fields, emancipate your negroes, and amalgamate the poor man's daughter and the rich man's buck-nigger before your very eyes !" *

It would be impossible to describe the excitement which this declaration of Mr. Curry produced. Of course the Congressman "ought to know."

Shortly after this remark had been made, I requested Mr. Curry to permit me to interrupt the thread of his discourse, just to make a short statement. The *honorable* gentleman audibly consented. I arose, and turned my face toward the audience with the words "Fellow-citizens !"

---

* See page 197.

At a signal from the chief of the Secret Association, of which Mr. Curry was indisputably an honored member, a sudden yell shook the building to its foundation. Every species of noise, and in almost every degree of intensity, pervaded the hall. The clamor was increased by the Bell and Douglas men, who shouted encouragingly to their Union representative. I fully expected Mr. Curry to relieve me of all embarrassment by explaining the facts. But the assistant precipitator, eager for applause, and ignoring his permission just given, remained imperturbably silent.

Under the circumstances, I contented myself with silencing the most vociferous of my persecutors with my clenched fist, and sat down.

After the meeting was over, I dared any man in the town to say that he went into that meeting previously agreed to cry me down. No one responded, although Robert Clark was sufficiently alarmed to have been the man. This man, after having been the most conspicuous Secessionist in town during the Presidential canvass, backed down completely when the war actually commenced. His treason was not even extenuated by courage. He planted a little cotton, and so he left the *brave non-slaveholders*, whom he had helped to madden with false statements, to fight and die in order that *he* might lounge around Wetumpka and retail the news. I suppose he was *conscripted*, if he ever entered the army at all.

Shortly after the disgraceful affair just alluded

to, I was informed that there would be a meeting
for free discussion at Buyckville, a German settle-
ment about twelve miles from Wetumpka. As
such meetings were very rare, I made it my business to be present. I also wanted an opportunity
to expose the disunionism of John C. Breckenridge
and others, and hoped it would be accorded me.
On my arrival in the village, I perceived that I
had been cruelly deceived. I do not think my
informant had set a trap for me, but I found myself in the midst of a meeting of Breckenridgers,
who were assembled for the purpose of organizing
a club for their own party, and who were actually
in expectation of Breckenridge speakers from Wetumpka, who had engaged to be present.

As mere lookers-on in Vienna, there were present five " Bell-Everett men" and eleven " Douglas
men," total sixteen Unionists.

Having comfortably disposed of my horse and
buggy, I approached the tavern, which also drove
a dry-goods business, and, saluting the crowd,
soon found myself in conversation with an old
acquaintance, William Speigner, who informed me
of my mistake, but insisted I should speak before
the crowd, saying that he would manage it.

A stranger approached us, was introduced as a
Bell man, and left us to make arrangements.

There was a slight board partition only between
us and several practitioners at the *bar* in the next
room. The following conversation was therefore
audible :

" Did you see Bob Tharin drive up ?"

" Ya-as."

" Do you think he'll speak ?"

" Dunno."

" But *I* know he *won't*, d—n him !"

" Why not ?"

" Bekase he's a d—d traitor !"

" You don't tell !"

" T' be sure. He's the very man we hollered down at Wetumpky t' other day, and we kin do it agin, I reckon."

" Go in, Pete, I'm along !"

" Hello ! Jo, come in here !"

An outside voice answered, " Hello !"

The outsider became an insider. I heard him enter, when he was thus addressed by the first speaker :

" Jo, *you* ain't for lettin' Tharin speak, ayre you ?"

" Yes ! most emphatically, I *am !*"

" Well, I ain't !"

" Why ?"

" Bekase he was hollered down at Curry's meetin' at Wetumpky."

" Well ! what of that ?"

" D— me if I want to listen to his d— Union stuff."

" Pete, you're a fool. The way to make people want to hear the man is to talk as you do. I am for letting him git up to talk, and then—"

Here followed a whispered conversation, when,

6*

with a roar of laughter, the three, having imbibed a last drink, went toward the school-house, which rose dilapidated in its vine-clad grotto, not far off.

Soon the "Bell man" returned with the invitation for me to go with him to the "academy."

As I drew near the building, I heard the president of the "club," announce my presence and my willingness to speak.

It was too late to recede.

The throng consisted principally of strangers to me, but those who knew me acknowledged the acquaintance. I could easily tell every Breckenridger present from the expression of malignant hate, or sinister triumph, which sat on the countenance of each. By my own party and by the Douglas men, I was received with the most marked consideration. A few moments more, and I found myself facing the crowd and ejaculating "Fellow-citizens."

I had already proved that the territorial question was a mere abstraction to at least fifteen out of sixteen of the inhabitants of Alabama, even if, as was not the case, the territories were at all fitted by climate for slavery, and was deliberately weighing the Union, with its countless blessings to the poor white men—the majority—the *people* *North* and *South* who owned no slaves, against the paltry selfishness of the few aristocrats and their transatlantic allies, who were about to precipitate the Cotton States into a bloody revolution, in order to gratify an unholy lust for power.

Suddenly a man in the crowd bawled:

" There ain't no Union now !"

The crowd here commenced shouting " that's so !" and, for some moments, nothing else could be heard.

Waiting patiently until the storm should subside, I replied:

" When that declaration shall be true—as it would never be if I could prevent it—no more will man be civilized or free. The despots of the Old World will reinstate their empire over the New ; the Lion of England will again roar in our forests, and her whelps will make lairs of our cotton fields and cities; the oppressed of this country will seek asylums in other climes, and Liberty will sink beneath a thousand blows. When your declaration shall be true, sir, freedom of speech will be but a name, and, *just in proportion as the Republic shall drift toward the maelstrom of dissolution*, will *American citizens* be insulted, their dearest privileges be invaded, and the right of speech be trampled upon by infuriated mobs. Yes, sir, when there shall be no more Union, the ' Cotton States' will become but a ' cotton patch' of England, over which will reign her ' viceroy,' in the person of John C. Breckenridge, or of William L. Yancey."

Here the Bell and Douglas men, who hate

Yancey, as the author of all the trouble, commenced a vociferous applause.

The president of the " Breckenridge Club" here remarked :

" Mr. Tharin, you have gone off in circumgyrations of eloquence; but you have not yet told us the remedy for Southern wrongs. Will you be pleased, as you are a native of Charleston, South Carolina, to tell us what you think ought to be done by the South."

." With pleasure, sir. ' The South,' however, is rather a general term, and includes a great many elements. *You*, sir, have, probably, one idea of the meaning of ' the South,' and *I* have, probably, another. I will proceed to define the term 'South,' according to the idea which I have received of it :

" ' The South,' when applied to the slaveholding section of the United States, signifies six millions of white and three millions of black inhabitants, by the census of 1850. The blacks are divided into ' field-hands, house-servants, and *mechanics*.' The whites are divided into slave-owners and non-slave-owners ; the slave-owners or cotton-planters are divided into lawyers, doctors, and office-holders ; and the non-slave-owners are divided into ' field-hands' and mechanics, with here and there a professional man snubbed by the planters and neglected by his own class.

" According to the last census (1850), which, being compiled by a native of Charleston, who is a resident of New Orleans, J. B. D. De Bow, is to

be relied on by us as containing nothing adverse
to Southern taste, and which I now hold in my
hand, the whole population of the United States
was in 1850, about twenty-three millions and fifty-
eight thousand, of whom nine millions six hundred
and twelve thousand, nine hundred and seventy-
nine are in the South; by the same statist the number of slave-owners in the whole South (and elsewhere in the Union) is three hundred and forty-
seven thousand, five hundred and twenty-five,
while the balance of the white population in the
South is six millions one hundred and eighty-four
thousand, four hundred and seventy-seven. We
will suppose that the whole increase of the white
population of the South is confined to the slave-
owners, in order to make the latter attain the
number of five hundred thousand, or half a mil-
lion, and *supposing the non-slaveholders to have
increased nothing*, we have them still numbering
over six millions.

"Thus I have proved, from the admission of
a native of Charleston, a resident of New Orleans,
a graduate of the same college, and a member of
the same literary society (the Cliosophic) as myself, that *the non-slaveholders of the South are at
least twelve times as numerous as the slaveholders.*
If we take Alabama herself, we will see that there
are over fourteen persons who have no negroes to
one who does own them. In *this* county, I venture to say, that there are at least *thirty* non-slaveholders to one slaveholder.

"Taking the census of Alabama, we find that there are, in Alabama, only thirty thousand slave-holders; that is to say, about the population of Mobile. The white population of Alabama is put down at over four hundred thousand; this makes the non-slave-owners fourteen times as numerous as the slave-owners.

"If Alabama be divided into fifteen cities, about the size of Mobile, the non-slave-owners will have fourteen of them, the slave-owners only *one!* In my native South Carolina the proportion is even more marked.

"Now, we begin to understand what the term SOUTH means, as to the *inhabitants* of the South; but we have not yet fully defined it. The South consists of fifteen States, the smallest of which contains an area equal to all Greece. Without particularizing, I will come right down to our own dear Alabama, whose wonderful wealth, not yet half realized, or even understood, is destined to make her the great emporium of the Gulf of Mexico, and whose central railroad, just under way, will, when completed, give her an opportunity to dispose of the vast beds of iron and of copper, of gold and of coal, which enrich her subterranean recesses. (Applause.) On my way hither, a distance of only twelve miles, I beheld the evidences of mineral wealth scattered all around me. We have all the facilities, also, for the culture of the grape; our streams are remarkable, even on this continent of great rivers, for their number, navi-

gability, and water-power; our vine-bearing hill-
sides gush out in medicinal springs; our ' valleys
also stand so thick with corn that they laugh and
sing.' Yes, my Alabamians, our State is the rich-
est, our rivers the grandest, our land the greenest,
our skies the brightest, our climate the sweetest,
our girls the loveliest, our boys the bravest in the
world—(prolonged applause)—and our non-slaveholding population who constitute the *people* of
Alabama, irrestrainable in the sublime upheavings
of our volcanic patriotism—ever ready to avenge
even a *fancied* insult from a *non-resident majority*
—(wild and vociferous applause)—will not always
omit to aim a crushing blow at the head of that
fleecy usurper who now looms up *in our very
midst* to crush us into the dust!"—

Here a commotion sprang up in the furthest end
of the " academy" between two persons:

" He *shall* speak!"

" He *shan't!* I'll kill him! he lies! That ain't
the way for a Southerner to speak!"

" Mister!" I exclaimed, " can't *you* wait until
I'm through, before you begin?"

Amid great laughter the " president" arose, his
lips quivering with fury, and demanded:

" How much more steam have you got on board?"

" Enough to burst your boiler and leave it as
empty as your head!"

The storm of derisive laughter which ensued
was very gratifying to the speaker, but *not* very
pleasing to my interrupter, who sat down so sud-

denly as to add a new element to the already vociferous mirth.

When order was restored, I proceeded thus:

"I was saying, when so harmlessly interrupted
(laughter) that the people of Alabama are too
brave even to permit the appearance of an insult
from a non-resident majority (applause). Would
to God, I could say as much for them in their intercourse with that *resident minority* who, enjoying all the offices of profit or of trust, dominate
over them with an iron hand! (Great confusion
and voices, which I did not stop for.) Would to
God that I could say cotton was discrowned!"

Of course, I was here interrupted. The sixteen
Unionists seemed completely *nowhere* in the row
that ensued; they hung their heads in shame, as
much as to say, "There now! he's gone and done
it." In the midst of the row, a man with a stick
exclaimed:

"Oh, you traitor! oh, you cuss, you!"

"Traitor! did *you* say *I* was a traitor, sir?"
("*Yes I did!!!*") "That same word was used to
the immortal Patrick Henry, when he said in the
Virginia Convention, that *George the Third, who
had an ear to hear*, might have his power overthrown in America. The man who called Patrick
Henry a traitor was himself an infamous *tory*, and
the man who says that *I* am a traitor, when I denounce 'King Cotton,' who, having *no* ear to be
appealed to by his trampled subjects, is a greater
tyrant than King George III., why, that man is

worse even than a tory. King George had some color of title to govern the colonies, but what title has 'King Cotton' to rule Alabama, to mob Southern men, to trample 'Southern Rights' into the dust, and to send his emissaries here even to interrupt and insult *me*, a Southern man, because I call upon my oppressed countrymen to be free? O Alabama! proud and glorious Alabama! rise from the ashes of thy desolation! declare thy independence of that single plant, which, monopolizing the whole surface of thy soil, shuts up thy recesses from the industry of thy children; wash off the stain of Secession from thy symmetrical limbs in thy beautiful streams, and, under the star-spangled banner, defy the Yanceys and the Breckenridges to rivet thy chains forever upon thee!

" Would to God that 'Southern Rights' could be respected by *Southern men ;* that every possible facility could be afforded for Alabama's full development; then we would not have *negro-equality forced upon us by a resident minority,* who now perform the almost entire labor of the State with their *black* field-hands and mechanics, and thus make four hundred thousand slaves drive five hundred thousand freemen from the culture of the soil, from the work-bench, from the factory, and from that personal equality, without which ' *State* equality' is but the shadow of a shade!"

Here several planters abruptly left the academy and gathered under trees outside of the building.

" I was asked what remedy against Southern

7

wrongs, I, as a South Carolinian, would advocate. South Carolina, gentlemen, has no right to dictate a policy to Alabama, any more than Massachusetts has. *Nor has Massachusetts any right to dictate a policy to South Carolina.* We are here as Alabamians, and as an adopted citizen of Alabama, of which my wife and child are natives, I answer the gentleman's question:

"The best remedy for 'Southern wrongs' is the vindication of 'Southern rights'—not alone the rights to power and influence of the minority whose cotton and niggers and plantations protect their rights but too well—but the rights of the poor white man, who owns no niggers, who owns no cotton, who owns no plantation, but in whose veins courses the same red stream which bled on the battle-fields of 1776, to give its descendants the blessings of freedom and equality. In order to do this I would

"1. Let perfect liberty of speech prevail! Let no more mobs prevent me, or other Southern men, from advocating 'Southern Rights' as *we* understand them.

"2. Let the *majority* of the people rule their State of Alabama *in* the Union; and let not a contemptible power-loving resident minority ' precipitate the Cotton States into a revolution,' which can but end in the perpetual degradation of the majority. (Applause by the Bell and Douglas men.)

"3. Let every demagogue who preaches disunion be avoided as a madman, and let King Cotton be consigned to the walks of private life, throneless and crownless, and co-equal with the other trees of the field.

"4. *Let the niggers be confined to the cotton field*, let no more negro blacksmiths, and negro carpenters, and negro bricklayers, and negro wheelwrights be used to drive the poor white man to poverty and to idleness, that root of all evil.

"Then, and not till then, will Alabama be herself. Then, and not till then, will the proper remedy be applied, as against Southern wrongs.

"You see, I am a *Southern Rights man* in the broadest sense. I interfere with no man's rights. I advocate the rights of all! Of course, I am not indifferent to my own blood-bought rights. Indeed, as a Southern man, I cannot permit others— whether they be Northerners or Southerners—to invade my own. When I was admitted to practice law in this very county, only fourteen miles from here, I recorded *an oath*. Now, *what* was that oath? Was it to support King Cotton?"—

Here an old gentleman, whose manners had evinced great delight at my whole speech, and who had been my most constant applauder, said, with great glee:

"No, it wan't!" (laughter.)

I continued: "Was it to support John C. Breckenridge?"

"No! siree!!" (laughter.)

"Were you there, sir?"

"I wan't nothin' else."

" Did you hear me take the oath ?"

" Yes; and I saw you *sign* it too !"

" Was it to support William L. Yancey ?"

" Not a bit of it."

" Well, what *was* my oath, sir ?"

" You swore to support the Constitution of Alabama."

" Was that all ?"

" No : you swore to support the Constitution of the United States."

" Have I done so to-day ?"

" Ef *you* haint, *nobody* ever did."

Here the Bell and Douglas men commenced to applaud ; and even the Breckenridgers seemed to think it a plain case,—and joined the others.

" Yes, sir, I keep my oath to-day, yesterday, and forever. *That oath is registered in heaven!* I make no light and foolish vows. That oath I intend to keep *always*, and, if I lose all the tranquillity and peace of mind I possess, *that* oath shall never, at God's bar, reproach *me*—as it will yet reproach many *other lawyers* and officers of Alabama—with perjury.

" In conclusion : *what* I have said, I have said in strict accordance with ' SOUTHERN RIGHTS !' If I have the misfortune to differ with men of wealth and influence, it shall, at least, never be said of R. S. Tharin that he was *afraid* to give a reason for the faith that is in him.

" I thank you for your attention."

After the speech was over, not a solitary insult

was leveled at me. The Bell and Douglas men gathered around me in a manner which showed their intention to protect my (Southern) rights. Around my buggy they arranged themselves. The president of the Breckenridge club approached with a crest-fallen countenance.

" Mr. Tharin, I am sorry I acted as I did, sir. I never interrupted a speaker before."

" Considering it was the *first* time, you managed it very well for a new beginner." This was said by a Douglas man, whose *size* was of itself an argument.

" If I only knew it to be your *last* attempt at so unworthy a pastime, I could not only forgive it, but forget it, sir."

A preacher here came up and said that he would like to discuss the question on the stump with me at any time I should appoint. I told him that I would leave it to my friends to appoint any time, and that I would be happy to meet him, provided there were *no interruptions*. On these terms, of course, the *reverend* mobocrat saw fit never to make arrangements.

But the most stormy elections must come to a conclusion. The contest ended quite too soon for Alabama's interests. Had the campaign lasted two months longer, Bell and Everett would have had a large majority, and she would afterward have refused to be "precipitated" into a foolish and a bloody revolution.

It was generally known that Abraham Lincoln

7*

was elected. The Secessionists exulted in his elevation, because they had planned and now claimed it as an argument in favor of Secession. Governor Moore, according to the programme of the conspirators, called a convention. It is not necessary here to state that the convention was called in order to "precipitate" Alabama out of the Union. Just on the eve of the assembling of the convention, I published my protest against indecent haste and the misrepresentation of the public opinion of the State, and proposed that the convention, when convened, should proffer to Alabama's sister States, North and South, a *National Convention*, for the purpose of amending the Constitution of the United States in certain important particulars, unnecessary to be enumerated here. Previous to that letter, I had addressed one, through the columns of the Montgomery *Confederation*, to a Dr. Wm. C. Penick, over my full signature, entitled "THE LIBERTY OF SPEECH," in which it was proved that the right of speech and the liberty of the press had been entirely destroyed by the unparliamentary and unconstitutional surveillance which the secret societies of traitors and Breckenridge clubs had been too long holding over Union meetings, Union speeches, and Union men. In this letter was shown the tendency of mobocracy, and the people were warned against the reign of terror, which ensued so shortly afterward, and of which I myself was soon to be among the most persecuted victims.

When the election of delegates to the Alabama State Convention was approaching, I announced myself the INDEPENDENT UNION CANDIDATE for a seat in that body, and would have been triumphantly returned from Coosa county, had it not been for the contemptible tricks of the Wetumpka branch of the Secret "League of United Southerners," of which the main society, at Montgomery, was presided over by the notorious Wm. L. Yancey.*

Finding that the secret "Committees of Safety," all over the South, were too much for my unassisted efforts, which only provoked ridicule, on account of the isolation of my opposition, I determined to organize "Committees of Safety" for myself and for the non-slaveholders, to rescue whom from the perpetual serfdom of a Cotton-Planters' Confederacy was (and is) my design. I solemnly devoted myself to the defence of *true* "Southern Rights." While I despised the insolent usurpations of the cotton nobility, I loved, while I pitied, the non-slaveholding whites, whose only hope in this world was the overthrow of King Cotton.

Although not, by birth and descent, a non-slaveholder, I was one of them at the time I speak of. I knew that *never*, in Congress, in State legislatures, in conventions,—whether political or commercial, State, sectional, or national,—had the non-

---

* See the Slaughter Letter, p. 212, in a note. Mr. Y. argued for "Committees of Safety."

slaveholders, as a class, had any—the slightest—
representation. On the contrary, by the aggressive
usurpations of the planters, we had been doomed
to a condition, as a class, but little, if any, above
the negroes themselves. The dominant class, possessing *unshared* legislative sway, easily excluded
these, the *people* of the South,—under the insulting
epithet of " poor white trash,"—from educational
and social advantages, until the mere mechanical
operation of choosing which slaveholder, or *cotton-
planter*, should *mis*represent us, was all that was
left us. The whole point is conceded in the term
which the planters used to describe the *modus* of
Secession. " *We*," wrote Yancey to Dr. Slaughter.
" We"—the planters of course—" will *precipitate*
the Cotton States into a *revolution*." This, he said
was to be accomplished by " organizing committees of safety all over the Cotton States—firing the
Southern heart, and giving courage to each other."
At first, electing Night to preside over their deliberations, they shrouded themselves in mystery ;
but, as the conspiracy culminated, after the conspirators had armed themselves with guns, stolen
from the unsuspecting government, they became
less reticent, and less guarded, and the Unionists
found themselves overpowered and subjugated,
even before many of them fully understood the
signs of the times. What are mere numbers without organization and without arms, where a small
proportion of the population, *armed, disciplined, organized, and aggressive*, hang like a thunder-cloud

over the country. "Southern Rights" were menaced then, from *within*. A *resident minority* had obtained the mastery. The indolence of unpreparedness weighed down the feeble knees of the multitude, and the only way to help ourselves, was to organize, as our enemies had done, *in secret*. But I was not destined to succeed, at *that* time, with my righteous undertaking. Whether I shall *ever* succeed in organizing my enslaved white brethren of Alabama and of the South is known only to Omniscience!

The secret societies commenced, at length, to show their transparencies in Wetumpka. Haggerty Hall began to be illuminated at a very late hour, and as the conspirators became less secret, resounded with the tread of armed military companies. The next move was to "enlist" *outsiders* "to meet the invading hosts of the damned Abolitionists!" No means were neglected to "fire the Southern heart." Tales of insurrectionary plots were bruited about the country, and the most ridiculous alarm created in unsuspecting bosoms. Then came those terrible associations,—the inevitable outgrowth of all mobocracies,—associations of proscription! The vigilance committee, the "committee of safety," and the Breckenridge club,* by an almost imperceptible transition, degenerated into the Jacobin clubs of a new "reign of terror,"

---

* The Breckenridge club in Alabama was not, of course, the same kind of club as the Breckenridge club *North*.

in which he who would not insult the American
flag, was considered amenable to the mob, which
was incited to its brutal acts by the diabolical
leaders of the secret associations. In every community sprung up some Robespierre,—some scent-
er of human blood; and to be suspected of *Lincolnism*—their new name of *Unionism*—was to
suffer,—generally *to die!* How lamentable for
the sacred cause of the Union that Mr. Lincoln
should have intensified this feeling and weakened
our hopes!

All this time my secret league of Union men
was slowly finding its way to the few; but I was
alarmed at the thought that I had commenced *too
late.* Still I persevered; but such was the jealousy
with which the villagers regarded my movements,
that I was reduced to temporary inaction.

Every now and then, by way of inspiring a
wholesome terror in the minds of Unionists, the
Breckenridge club of Wetumpka would denounce
and mob some defenseless person. The victim of
this persecution, who did not immediately recant,
was tarred and feathered, hanged, shot, or acci-
dentally committed suicide. The club denounced
a poor illiterate jeweler, William S. Middlebrooks,
whose only alleged offence was " being a Lincoln-
ite!" The *modus operandi* would, doubtless, be
not uninteresting.

SCENE THE SECOND.

"SOUTHERN RIGHTS."

"To bear affronts too great to be forgiven,
And not have power to punish!"

On the eastern bank of the Coosa river (a trib-
utary of the Alabama), where it flows through
the village of Wetumpka, stands a small square
brick building, containing but two apartments,
and dignified by the euphonious appellation of
the "Calaboose." Herein are incarcerated incor-
rigible negroes, or belligerent countrymen, who
become riotous over the fruits of their exchanges
with the stores, which barter for raw produce or
sell for cash the calicoes, shoes, hats, or whisky,
desired by their customers.

On a stormy night, whose impenetrable darkness afforded an appropriate vail for the deed of
rascality about to be perpetrated, a low-lived
white man, Bob Clark, sneaked up to the only
window of the calaboose, and, putting his lips to
the grating, whispered—

"Sam!"

No answer being elicited, the monosyllable was
repeated in louder and louder tones, until, from

the floor, a sleepy grunt, well perfumed with bad whisky, was emitted in a guttural

"Who dat?"

"Hush! Listen! Can you tell me, Sam, who would be a good person to leave some Lincoln-powder with?"

"Wha' sort o' powder dat?"

"*Lincoln*-powder—powder to shoot white men with and make niggers free!" *

"Who be you? Wha' fur you gwine do dat ting? You better take care ob youself, talkin' sich tings to niggers? *Who* you be?"

"Never mind, Sam, I'm a friend. Do you think, Sam, that William S. Middlebrooks would be a safe man to leave some with?"

"What I know 'bout it? Lef dis nigger 'lone! Dono nuffin 'bout it, 'tall. S'pose Mr. Middlebrooks would do 'bout as well as *me*. Yah, yah, yah!"

This was all that was necessary to fasten suspicion upon poor Middlebrooks. I am glad I am not master of invective strong enough to characterize adequately the perpetrator of *such* an act.

The next morning, as I was returning to my law-office, I saw consternation written upon the faces of almost all the people I met. Caution had already become necessary in all Union men, and conversation between them was, by tacit consent, waived in the presence or hearing of Disunionists.

---

* Alas, how *prophetic* were those words of a traitor!

Besides this, the pieces I had published in the Montgomery *Confederation*, over my own signature, had rendered me an object of ill-disguised hatred to the partisan disunion demagogues of the town. It was, therefore, getting more and more unfashionable to be seen in my company, unless on business. But although on that morning no word was spoken by them, the faces of my friends were full of communications, and their eyes seemed to appeal to mine to know what ought to be done.

That some "Secession devilment" had been perpetrated, and that, too, of a bolder and more tyrannical character than usual, even in that latitude, was too evident to be doubted.

Not many minutes elapsed after my arrival at my office before a timid knock was heard at the door. It opens, and a friend, whose present and future safety render it improper to mention his name, entered, with—

"Have you heard the news?"

"No; but I perceive there must be something startling by the manners of the people. What's up now?"

"Promise me that, for your own safety and the safety of the cause, you will *not* acquiesce in the request I promised to bear you!"

"If I view acquiescence dangerous to myself and to the cause of the Union, I will refuse it."

"Good! Then I will proceed to tell you something startling. As I was passing over the

8

bridge, a sound of terror filled my ears, while appeared, at the other end of the structure, a packed mass of howling humanity. From the center of the crowd towered the gleaming bayonets of the Wetumpka Light Guard. Upon their nearer approach, I perceived in their midst *a white man bound between two negroes,* the three dragged along as prisoners in the hands of their unauthorized captors. He was borne to the Wetumpka Bastile (Haggerty Hall), where he is now confined. I soon met his frantic wife, who was following the maltreaters of her husband. I asked her what was the matter, when, collecting her scattered senses, she turned to me with a look I shall never forget, and said that she was on her way to your office, 'in order to get you to sue out the proper writ, and requested me to entreat you to befriend her husband."

" Certainly I will. Who is the prisoner?"

" William S. Middlebrooks."

" What! the jeweler?"

" Yes."

" What's the charge?"

" L-i-n-c-o-l-n-i-s-m!"

" *What's that?*"

" Don't know. Some *pretext* of the secret association."

" Why Middlebrooks is a *Douglas democrat!*"

" True; but his enemies are numerous. You know his business improves lately, while the business of McKonichy, the Secessionist, diminishes.

It is mighty easy, it seems, for these disunion devils to break up any man, these days!"

" This is outrageous! I can't see how the safety of the *Union*, or even *my own*, can be affected, by my befriending this injured American citizen!"

" *Your* enemies are even more numerous and more vindictive than *his* enemies. You would sooner or later be mobbed, or assassinated; besides they will call you an Abolitionist, and thus your usefulness and your *days* will be brought to a simultaneous close."

" But have I not in open court, when admitted to practice law in Alabama, taken and recorded a solemn oath to support the Constitutions of the United States and of the State of Alabama, *both* of which have been palpably violated this very morning? Did I not, at the same time, swear ' never, for considerations personal to myself, to neglect the cause of the defenseless and oppressed.'* Is not poor Middlebrooks ' defenseless and oppressed?'

" When Luther was informed that his enemies were numerous in Worms, and that he had better not go thither, he exclaimed: ' Were there in Worms, as many devils as there are tiles upon the housetops, I *will* enter the city!' This is not the first time that I have risked, and even sacrificed, popularity, for the maintenance of the non-slave-

---

* Section 732, Code of Alabama.

holder's rights, and I'll take this case, if I die for
it!"

"I was afraid you would! You are imprudent
—but you are *right!*"

The resolution once taken, I proceeded to arrange my plans.

The danger of the course determined on was,
by no means, inconsiderable. It was, in the excitement of the hour, suicide to make known my
determination.

But a thought suggested itself to my mind,
which was acted upon with promptness. I peti-
tioned the governor to command the "Wetumpka
Light Guard" to protect myself and client during
the prosecution of the cases about to be commenced.

It will be remembered that the Governor of
Alabama, Andrew B. Moore, had recorded an
oath to support the Constitution of the United
States and of the State, respectively, and that he
had also *sworn* "to see that the *laws* be *faithfully*
executed."

While awaiting an answer from the capitol,
only fourteen miles off, still another outrage was
committed, of, if any thing, a baser character than
the first.

Some youths, considering themselves as much
authorized to depredate as their mobocratic seniors,
visited the abode of the imprisoned Middlebrooks,
tore down his fences, insulted his wife, and would
have proceeded further; but the heroic woman

gave them to understand that she could and *would shoot*, when the terrified young rebels—*especially William Mc Williams—evacuated!*

It was determined to include these also in the suits at law which were preparing.

It being next to impossible to get a "summons and complaint" through the post-office, on account of the censorship of the mails, which was a part of the Secession system, it was found necessary to get the documents to the clerk of court through another channel.

Let me here intimate that Middlebrooks was discharged on the morning of the third day of his imprisonment. The consequence was that the writ of *habeas corpus* which had been commenced was never sent to the proper officer. In the State of Alabama this is the judge of probate of the county. He resided at Rockford, twenty-six miles of a difficult mountain road from Wetumpka.

"Had a *white* man," so decided the vigilance committee of Wetumpka, "said what Sam, the *negro*, said concerning Middlebrooks, the latter would have been *hanged;* but, for want of *white testimony*, he is discharged." This was not very complimentary to Bob Clark, but shows how easy it becomes for usurpers to dominate over Southern Rights!

The *answer* of the governor now arrived. No letter, no message to his legal correspondent, but an order to the Wetumpka Light Guard to proceed at once to Pensacola, *via* Montgomery.

There can be no doubt that my letter to Gov.
Moore was used by that perjured traitor for my
destruction instead of for my protection. Not
only was his withdrawal of the Wetumpka Light
Guard evidently so intended, but it is not at all
unlikely that the forsworn governor set his spies
and assassins on my path, because my intentions
toward Middlebrooks showed my devotion to the
poor white people whom his excellency despised
and aided to oppress.

Poor Middlebrooks, although no longer held
"in durance vile," was compelled to languish
under the law of public odium and disgrace, after
disgrace was heaped upon him, on account of a
mere captious suspicion. By an almost unanimous vote, he was expelled from the military company and left in the most humiliating condition.
This is always the case with the victim of unauthorized power. What redress has any man,
North or South, who is falsely arrested or imprisoned by ruffians and traitors?

True to my oath "to support the Constitution
of the United States, and the Constitution of *Alabama*, and *never, for considerations personal to
myself, to neglect the cause of the defenseless and
oppressed*," I had already prepared, in duplicate,
the "summons and complaint," which Alabama,
in her Code, has made and provided as the only
legal commencement of civil and criminal actions.
"False imprisonment" was, of course, the main
charge alleged, and the defendants consisted of the

most influential and wealthy of the planters of the community.

There was a double danger attendant upon mailing .the summons and complaint in Wetumpka. First, it would probably be ransacked at the post-office and withheld from the mail; and, next, my own danger would be, by no means, trifling.

My mother was, at the time, on a visit from my native Charleston, S. C., to Wetumpka. On her return toward Charleston, she was to .stop a few days, on a visit to her brother-in-law's family, at Collirene, Lowndes county, Alabama, and I determined to fulfill a long standing promise, and visit my relations in her company.

When I embraced my wife and little daughter at Wetumpka, a shadow fell upon my spirit—a shadow from that stormy interim, that was to intervene between that parting and our next meeting.

Little did either of us think the time was so near. Three or four months from that parting, the husband and wife, and their *two* children, met at Cincinnati, which neither of them had ever seen before.

How appropriate it is that a loyal husband should enjoy the society of a loyal wife! The former risks his life for the Union—the latter leaves her mother and her childhood scenes, her brothers pressed into the Southern army, the remains of her sacred dead, and cleaveth unto her husband.

The reflections which passed through my mind, as I sat with my mother in the cabin of the steamer, which was "coughing down the river" in the manner peculiar to river-craft, were of a varied character. About three years before that night, I had alighted from the stage at the "Coosa Hall," a stranger to the ways of Alabama. Full of that high-toned feeling which I then denominated "Southern chivalry," I had entered upon my duties as a teacher with a high regard for the nobleness of the profession, and not without a secret delight at the feeling of having "all the world before me, where to choose." For many months after I had arrived in Wetumpka, my popularity had increased. The young of both sexes had courted my society. The old had commended and caressed me. In the parlors of the citizens I was ever a welcome guest. My friends were everywhere, and my enemies nowhere. Among the beautiful daughters of the village I found a paradise of innocent recreation. I did not think to proclaim to all the world that I owned no cotton; for in the innocence of my heart I supposed they all knew it sufficiently well. But I was, unknown to myself, floating upon a treacherous stream. The roses which supported my reclining limbs were all artificial. Let me illustrate:

From the air of city-life, which I brought with me from the "Queen city of the South," the rustic population of Wetumpka had formed the idea,

" he must be *rich*." Never to mortal had I ever
breathed that I was, or was not rich. The idea
had been born of their own good wishes, or else
of their sordid desires, concerning me.

Among the ladies of Wetumpka was one whom
I sometimes met in company, and sometimes
visited at her cottage home not far from the banks
of the Coosa. The good sense, the modesty, the
goodness, which illuminated her life, made their
impression upon me, as they had universally impressed all who had ever had the pleasure to know
her. Graceful and dignified, she participated, like
some superior being, in the gay scenes around her.
The cup of pleasure, which others too eagerly, or
too noisily quaffed, she sipped with a retiring gen-
tleness, which, all unconsciously to herself, was
the passport to many a youthful heart.

From the gorgeous temples of affluence, and
their bejeweled daughters, I began to steal away
to the cool freshness of her moonlit piazza, to
listen, with her, to the mockbird's evening hymn,
and to a voice more sweet than even his, which,
in all ages of the world, has had its entranced lis-
teners. Insensibly to ourselves, our hearts melted
into one, and our hands soon followed the example. On the 20th of April, 1858, I led her to
the altar a blooming bride, and never has she
given me cause to regret the most happy act of
my life.

The unostentatious manner in which we commenced our married life, soon removed the scales

from the eyes of those who had supposed I "must be rich," and a most marked change became visible in the little world of my wife's native town.

The true condition of things began to dawn upon me. We were non-slaveholders! We had preferred each other's society to the plantations and negroes, which it is almost invariably the grand object of Southern marriage to secure. Having disdained to ally myself, by marriage, to King Cotton, I was soon to experience the "slings and arrows of outrageous fortune." Men, who had looked up to me as their oracle, in politics, in literature—I write without egotism, for to be *their* oracle was not much, to be sure—began to detract from my real merits as much as they had once overrated them. One of these, whose unholy ambition it was to "*marry a plantation*," and who, after many efforts, had at length succeeded, although his conduct confessed that it had an encumbrance—an unloved wife—was particularly marked in his opposition to myself. His plantation, in one week after he obtained it, had made him monarch of all he surveyed. I shall not mention his name; but, if he ever reads this book, he will recognize his likeness in this description.

I never *envied* the planters of Wetumpka, or, indeed, of any part of the South. My *dislike* to them arose from their contemptible meanness, their utter disregard to common decency, their supercilious arrogance, and their daily usurpations of powers and privileges at variance with

my rights, and the rights of my class. No sooner
had I insulted their self-esteem by taking the case
of Franklin Veitch, than business deserted my
office, and an odium as unjust as it was, at the
time, inexplicable, pursued my steps. Even some
of those who should, by every tie of friendship
and of relationship by marriage, have sustained
my honorable course, had yielded to the popular
clamor, and *dared* not show their kindliness, if
they felt it. But I had not married the whole
family, although I felt bitterly the tame syco-
phancy which would pander to the mob, and
which, while it possessed every opportunity to
know the truth, would, nevertheless, "go with
a multitude to do evil."

After all I had suffered, there was still a tie
that bound me to Wetumpka. It was the native
place of my wife, and had been the scene of some
happy days to me. I hoped soon to return to it,
to clasp my family to my heart. It was not without a pang, and a fearful augury of evil, that I
felt myself receding from its "darkening shores."
I raised my eyes. My mother's sad and tearful
countenance met my view, her eyes resting upon
me with a commiserating glance that showed that
she had read my thoughts. In silence we drifted
down the Coosa, both of us thinking of the wonderful changes that had transpired in my destiny
since, three years before, I had parted from that
mother in Charleston, with hope in my eye and
elasticity in my step. We had not met once in

that three years, and now, on her return home-
ward, I could see that she experienced alarm for
the exposures I was subjected to, on account of
my uncompromising Unionism. She had come
lately from a city and from a State where Secession had flung around itself the folds of revolutionary drapery. What *everybody* said, she had
believed; but what a different view she must have
entertained of "Southern Rights," when her son
had to go to another county to mail the writ which
was intended to vindicate the inborn rights of an
ill-used Southern man!

After stopping an hour at Montgomery, which
was waving, even.then, with significant flags,
we continued our voyage until we arrived, at
about 10 P. M., at Benton, in Lowndes county,
where we disembarked, and waited for morning.
The next day we started in a team drawn by two
mules, and, sticking about a half-dozen times in
the heavy prairie mud, which rose above the hubs
of the wheels, by the help of levers of fence-rails
we "pried" ourselves out, and arrived, at length,
at our destination.

Nature never made a lovelier spot than Collirene
Hill. As the most dramatic event of my life took
place upon this arena, it may not be amiss to
give the reader a short description of its topog-
raphy.

Collirene Hill, or rather hills, must be conceived
of as an abrupt elevation on the Bentonward side,
stretching its summit, in the shape of a broad table

of land for about a square mile, in every direction around my uncle's home, except where a lovely little valley nestled behind his house into a field of several acres which he partially cultivated. To the crest of the hills, from the direction of Benton, the elevation is precipitous. Several fine houses of wood ornament the flat stretch of ground on its top, and the acerose pines twinkle their fronds in unbroken forests beyond the lowland plantations which lie *perdu* at their limits. The blacksmith shop of *Doctor* Dunklin, resounded on one side of the road, and my uncle's wheelwright shop was jammed in a hollow, on the other. In the former, the Doctor, a cotton-planter, of course, employed two stalwart black slaves, while in the latter my aged uncle shoved daily his laborious plane. Both the Doctor and the wheelwright would have blazed into frenzy had you told them *Edward Everett* was not for *negro-equality.* They had been both for *Breckenridge* in the last presidential canvass, and, so, they imagined they were the peculiar guardians of "Southern Rights." The Doctor by "Southern Rights" understood his own rights to employ black mechanics to the exclusion of his neighbor, the wheelwright; and the wheelwright, who had grown gray at his work-bench, understood, by "Southern Rights," the right of Doctor Dunklin to think as he pleased and act as he pleased in the premises.

Having mailed the writ to the clerk of court of Coosa county, and having addressed a letter to

9

my friend, Hon. Lewis E. Parsons, of Talladega, a
Douglas democrat, who was entreated to officiate,
should *accident* prevent the writer from being
present at the trial, I turned my attention to
the elements of which " Collirene Hill" was composed.

The little community of Collirene, on account
of its natural beauty, consisted almost entirely of
"planters." A few persons of the poorer class
existed among them, but their numbers were exceedingly small, and their influence smaller.

The wheelwright shop of my uncle, Daniel C.
Tharin, was frequented by the " chivalry" of the
neighborhood, who amused themselves by shooting at a tall board, hewn into the shape of a man,
and denominated " Old Abe." This crowd consisted of Col. Robert Rives, " Professor" Harris,
Dr. Dunklin, Dr. Dunklin Pierce, and others,
whose principal occupation, when they were not
shooting at " Old Abe," was the discussion of the
relative merits of Jeff. Davis, Bill Yancey, and
Alexander H. Stevens.   Dr. Dunklin Pierce having just returned from witnessing the inauguration
of Davis, at Montgomery, was full, to bursting,
with enthusiasm and "chivalry." Such was his
delight at the " success" of Secession, which, he
claimed, was insured by the inauguration of Jeff.
Davis, that he rushed toward the imperturbable
"Old Abe," and fired his navy-revolver six
times in rapid succession, without a single ball
coming out of the muzzle, although the smothered

reports were all heard. Upon examination, it was discovered that the weapon had burst at the side. This event brought an expression of dismal augury upon the face of the crowd. " Old Abe" seemed to chuckle inwardly at the *contre-temps*, as much as to say : " Young man, you are spared to die by a *halter*, not a fire-arm, while I am destined to outlive this miserable farce." The next time I heard the report of gunpowder in commemoration of a president's inauguration, was when, standing on the levee of Cincinnati, an exile as I was, a few weeks afterward, I heard the mighty voices of cannon announcing the accession to the presidential chair of the nation, of that man, who, once a conservative patriot, has had the folly to yield to the pressure of radicalism, and who, confused by the clash of arms, has forgotten his letter to Horace Greeley, wherein he promises that he " would save the *Union*." " Lincoln-powder" no longer means any thing. It should signify the " Union of our forefathers," it should mean that all who resist the restoration of the American Union, whether they swear by the Richmond *Examiner* or the New York *Tribune*, whatever be their motive, must be classed in the same black category of treason and of crime.

The would-be inauguration of Davis occurred on the 18th, or 19th of February, 1861. *The* dramatic scene of my life was, in a few days, to begin.

I had next to combat the long-standing preju-

dices and secession proclivities of my uncle. I
was very earnest in my advocacy of my correct
views of "Southern Rights." These views were
and are defensive of the white non-slaveholders of
the South; first, by restoring the Union through
their votes, by means of previous secret organization; and then, by confining slave-labor to the
cotton-fields exclusively, leaving the anvil and the
work-bench, and the trades of life under the control of the poor white population.

The *abuse* of the "peculiar institution," I argued, had overshadowed and destroyed *all* other
institutions of the country. The institutions of
free-press, free-speech, and *represented taxation*,
for which last the war of Independence had been
waged—where were they? The Legislature, which
framed the artful call for a Secession Convention
consisted *only* of cotton-planters, the representatives, *bonâ fide*, of cotton-planters, and therefore of *their* "peculiar institution." The perjured
governor of the State, himself a cotton-planter, of
course, had convoked the Legislature and, through
it, the Convention, for the avowed supremacy of
"King Cotton." The election of delegates to the
Convention was an insult to every man in Alabama who planted no cotton, who owned no slave,
or who *thought* he was a freeman. In almost
every county in South Alabama, the cotton-
planters permitted no one to be *nominated* who
did not support Secession. In middle and northern Alabama, the candidates were all secretly

agreed on precipitation. Cotton-planters *pro*, and cotton-planters *con*. The people elected Union men, as they thought, but the Union men voted disunion, according to previous agreement; and the people, accustomed to be "sold," were told that the measure was imperative to save Alabama from "*invasion*," and, in the next breath, promised them that Secession would be "*peaceable*." Coosa and Tallapoosa counties, adjoining each other, sent men to the Convention, who denounced Secession from every stump; and "pledged their counties to Secession," when overawed by the presence of King Cotton. Tom Wats—who "planted cotton" in Alabama and Texas, and who, by espousing the cause of Bell and Everett, had gained tremendous power in Alabama—showed *why* he had once advocated the "*Union*, the Constitution, and the enforcement of the laws." Mr. Yancey moved that the Secession flag (the *State* flag *he* called it) should be raised, each day at certain hours, from the dome of the State capitol. Tom Wats moved as an amendment, that it "float" therefrom "forever." My uncle listened with a saddened, but acquiescent expression, when I proved that the cotton-planters *alone* had gotten up this revolution and that they were preparing to rivet the chains which they had already thrown upon the *people* of the State.

These conversations I purposely held in the presence of some poor non-slaveholders, who loved the *Union*, and who, for the first time, had met

9*

one of its friends, who *dared* to vindicate it.
Gradually I began to suggest the repeal of the
ordinance of Secession by means of a secret society. A small, but patriotic association was the
result, to which my uncle declined to belong, but
which began to take form as an outpost of that
which I had already originated in Coosa county.
I denominated the Collirene Society, the "TRUE
SOUTHERN RIGHTS CLUB."

The purpose of this association was to "fight
fire with fire,"—to band together all who confessed other interests than those of "King Cotton,"
and, at the maturity of the plan, to elect a Union
governor, pledged to call a convention of the
people, and, by the votes of the non-slaveholding
population, to repeal the infamous ordinance of
Secession, which had been passed, as I have before
intimated, without the presence in Convention of
a single non-slaveholder, as the representative of,
by far, the most numerous class in the State—in
the United States—*in the world!*

But, there was a traitor in that devoted little
band, who, owning neither slave nor cotton, but
willing to sell his little soul for a nigger—and he
could not but have been the gainer in such a bargain—betrayed his birthright for a mess of pot-
tage.

John V. Buford, having become the recipient
of the Secret, and having become a subscriber to
the *Non-slaveholder*, which I was, in the fullness
of time, to have published in Montgomery, in ad-

vocacy of the rights of the "poor white trash," impeached me before the so-called "LEGAL VIGI-LANCE COMMITTEE OF COLLIRENE BEAT, LOWNDES COUNTY, ALABAMA," and, one fine morning, while at breakfast, I was informed that five gentlemen of the vigilance committee desired to see me.

At that dreadful announcement an ominous silence brooded over the scene. The suspended fork remained rigid in mid-air; the viand, un-tasted, was slowly redeposited upon the plate from which it had just been lifted; the distended eye glanced from face to face, only to grow more awe-struck from the view.

With compressed lip and beating heart, I said : "Ask them to walk in."

In a few moments the shuffling of feet in the passage and the moving of chairs in an adjoining room gave token of the commencement of an ordeal from which an escape was, at that period, an unrecorded phenomenon.

On my way from one room to the other, a lifetime of thought passed through my mind. *My oath*—Franklin Veitch, "defenseless and op-pressed"—William S. Middlebrooks, "oppressed and defenseless"—and now their unperjured champion—all three of us seemed clanking our chains in a vain chorus to assail the ear of nar-cotized Liberty. I could not feel my situation as keenly as prudence might require. My indigna-tion for a moment overpowered every other feel-ing, and I had to curb my wrath in order to enter

the room. My partial success was increased by
my mother's hand and voice, the one laid on my
shoulder, the other breathing in my ear—

"Robert! Robert! for *my* sake!"

I entered the room with outward composure.
The sub-committee, all strangers, exchanged salu-
tations with me, and a silence of several minutes
reigned throughout the apartment.

SCENE THE THIRD.

"THE VIGILANCE COMMITTEE."

"What are fifty, what a thousand slaves,
Matched to the sinews of a single arm
That strikes for liberty?"—*Brooke.*

" Mr. Tharin," said their spokesman, " we have
been appointed by the vigilance committee of this
beat to request your presence before them, because
of certain charges which have been laid against
you. The committee is now in session, awaiting
your presence, at the Old Academy."

I repressed an imprudent outburst of indignation, and then, in the calmest tones I could command, I asked—

" By what *authority* does a vigilance committee
summon a free-born *citizen* of Alabama before
them to answer *charges*, and *so forth ?*"

" By their *own* authority !" was the fierce and
insulting reply.

" A civil question deserves a civil answer. I
am about to show, sirs, that your vigilance committee has *no* authority in the premises, and that
its members lay themselves open to an action at
law."

" What use, Mr. Tharin, in arguing this question ? If you are innocent, you ought to have no objection to appear before any tribunal."

" That's so !" exclaimed the Hercules of the crowd, who sported an immense white cowhide, white pants, white hair, white eyebrows, eyelashes, eyes—the incarnation of his dreaded " king."

" That's so !" reiterated the others, in sycophantic chorus.

" It is *not* always right," I rejoined, " for innocent individuals to appear, at their summons, before every unauthorized tribunal.*   Innocence would be unavailing, if it did not exempt its possessor from illegal and unauthorized restraint. Even guilt is exempt from *illegal* arrest.

" Besides, gentlemen, *I have taken an oath to sustain the Constitution of Alabama, which denies to you such powers as you assume.*†

" Again : you believe in ' State sovereignty.' You would consider any man worthy of execration (and so do I) who would deny legitimate State sovereignty. ' State-sovereignty,' ' State-equality'

---

* In *any* section of my country, let me add.

† " No person shall be *accused, arrested,* or *detained,* except in cases ascertained *by law,* and *according to the forms* which the same has prescribed : and no person shall be punished but in virtue of a *law* established and promulgated *prior* to the offence and *legally* applied."—*Constitution of Alabama,* Art. I., § 2.

Also : " No person shall be deprived of life, liberty, or property, but by due course of law."—*Id.,* § 10.

—these are the great war-cries of the day. It is the very foundation-stone of the coming revolution. Now, on page 113, Hoffman's Chancery Practice, volume i., you will find substantially these words: ' A State is *not* sovereign, *unless* she afford perfect immunity to all her citizens against every species of arrest, except by her own officers and according to her own laws.' You are, therefore, invited, gentlemen, to produce your legal *warrant*, in the hands of a legal *officer*, containing a *specific charge*, and appointing a stated day of *public trial*, in the *proper place*, and by a jury of my peers.* To such an officer, and to no other, can I surrender the sacred person of an American citizen, consistently with my oath to support the Constitution of *Alabama*, consistently with my convictions of that personal equality, which is not inferior to even the State equality you boast, or consistently with that view of State sovereignty which *you* and *I* entertain, although from different points of view. With whatever force, therefore, an American citizen, claiming for his justification and protection the laws of his nation and the laws of his State, can enunciate such a conclusion, I must decline your invitation to answer ' charges' before the vigilance committee, which you, in part, represent."

---

* "The right of trial by jury shall remain inviolate."— *Constitution of Alabama*, Art. I., § 28.

"No power of suspending laws shall be exercised, except by the general assembly or its authority."—*Id.*, § 15.

"What are we to do, Tharin, with such doctrines, in times like these?"

"The revolutionary period in every country is *the* period most in need of the observance of constitutional law. The innocent could quite easily be made the victims of proscription, and even of *mobocratic violence*, were it not for the ægis of the sacred law, which was intended to shelter all persons in times like these, unless and *until* repealed by the proper authority. The laws which protect me are *beyond the reach of your vigilance committee, and even of change*, being '*forever*' excepted from all legislation *in futuro*, by the first article, or 'declaration of rights,' as it is called, of the Constitution of Alabama."*

"Gentlemen," cried their chairman, "we have been commanded to take this man, dead or alive, before the legal vigilance committee of Collirene Beat, Lowndes county, Alabama: we have accepted the commission. Shall we proceed at once to the discharge of our duties?"

The speaker and the "accused" simultaneously started to their feet, the former to offer, the latter to repel, violence. While thus they stood at opposite sides of the circle confronting each other, a voice struggled up through a cloud of cigar

---

* "Every thing in this article is excepted out of the general powers of government, and *shall forever remain inviolate,* and all laws *contrary* thereto shall be *void.*"—*Const. Ala.,* Art. I., part of § 30.

smoke in the corner, and Williams, the irate chairman, obeyed the injunction :

" Sit down, gentlemen."

The smoker then continued thus :

" No man can listen to Mr. Tharin and not be impressed with the fact that he has studied this whole question better than we have. But only to a certain extent, Mr. Tharin, will our course be imperative. Have you any suggestion, through us, to make to the vigilance committee ? If so, we can carry it up, unless the majority *here* dissent. If the latter, you *must* go, *nolens volens*."

The prisoner (for such evidently I was), after a moment's reflection, said :

" If the vigilance committee will resolve themselves into an assemblage of citizens, *without organization*, I will *address* them on subjects of interest which occupy the universal mind."

A majority of the sub-committee were found willing to carry up the proposition, and, leaving a guard over their prisoner—their prisoner in *avowed* defiance of all law—national, *State*, and even CONFEDERATE—the others departed.

Four hours of keenest suspense elapsed, and the committee of five reassembled to inform the prisoner that his proposition was acceded to by a majority of—three !

The uncle of the accused, who had formerly been a member of the vigilance committee, and who remained present, as a member, so long as he thought good might be effected, when the small majority of *three* was reported in favor of a measure which, conscience dictated, ought to have received unanimous approbation,—resigned!

Poor old man! He had never been of th**è**m, although with them.

He declared himself "ashamed" of having been, at any time, a member of so merciless and unauthorized a body of men. He reported afterward, that knives and revolvers were freely drawn in the heat of debate, and that not a few insisted that the only balsam for the wounded dignity of the vigilance committee, would be the unconditional surrender of the person of the accused. But, by the most cunning brains present, it was urged that they did not know how large a party in other counties Mr. Tharin might have; that, since he had appealed to *law*, a seeming acquiescence on their part would disarm popular objection and forestall organized opposition; that he was an outspoken man, and would implicate himself before the assembly he had convoked, by defending, instead of denying his acts and opinions, and that their future course, *as an organization*, would be based upon his admissions in his speech, which were sure to be on the side of the Union, and hostile to the "Confederate States of America."

In custody of his guard (it is best to call things by their right names), in custody of his *guard* the "orator of the day" advanced into the midst of his enemies, saluting the few whom he knew, and compressing under his arm the Code of Alabama

and Hoffman's Chancery Practice, the former of
which contained (contains!) enough to consign to
the penitentiary, or to a fine of one thousand dollars, one or both, each of the party who had already invaded his rights by bringing him before
an unauthorized body.

The eyes of that crowd of semi-barbarians involuntarily turned upon the slight figure, who,
walking through their midst, entered the building,
in and *around* which they were assembled. Numbers were too much enraged to enter the apartment;
but *all heard* what followed. The largest part of
the crowd was without.

The glances of the Unionist traveled around the
host of his enemies. The very large majority of
youths, the general expression of their countenan-
ces, were unfavorable indications. The building
was small, the seats consisting of loose boards
laid over pine logs, and at right angles with
them.

The horses of the crowd were tied by their
bridles to swinging limbs on the skirts of the hill.
Their stolid indifference was in marked contrast
to the interest—the excitement—of the human
brutes in their vicinity.

The day was lovely, the air transparent, revealing, far out through the sentinel pines that line
the summit of "Collirene Hill," one of the most
Eden-like countries on the globe. Here and there,
from the lovely valley rose grouped or solitary
hills, embosomed in fields just losing the russet of

winter in the buds of early spring. In that valley, as in countless others in that State, slumbered
the unappropriated wealth of inexhaustible mines
and quarries of almost every species of metalifer-
ous and rupiferous deposit. Fountains of medicinal value gushed from the gorgeous hill-sides—
"*vitiferi colles*"—which, at the proper season,
presented their luscious clusters to unrealized
vintages. Above them all, obscuring the purple
sky, towered the colossal, almost palpable form
of " King Cotton," who, monopolizing with despotic sway the whole *surface* of the earth, locked
up her *recesses* from the miner's shaft, the geolo-
gist's hammer; denouncing all such " new-fangled
notions" as among the " encroachments of the
North."

The Unionist was disagreeably aroused from
his reverie, which had not consumed the time
necessary for this allusion, by the harsh voice of
Williams:

" Mr. Tharin is present," he announced, " and
I move that Dr. Dunklin take the chair."

The motion was carried, *nemine contradicente.*

The " object" of the meeting having been suc-
cinctly stated by the chairman, at once the most
passionless, the most unscrupulous, the most intelligent, and, *therefore*, the most *degraded* of *that*
assembly, " Mr. Tharin, was permitted to speak,
but to speak to the point, without preface or cir-
cumlocution."

" Mr. Chairman : According to the *permission*

of this assembly I am here to *speak*—perhaps to *die!* I know not and—were it not for my family, whom God preserve—I care not which; for I have lived to see the day in American history when whosoever would save his life—all that makes life endurable in the pursuit of true happiness—shall lose it; when truth must be spoken with cautious smoothness; when freedom of speech—*once* a right of American citizens, and still theoretically granted all over the land—must be begged as a boon, is extended as an unmerited favor, and received as an undeserved privilege; when secret associations—"

Now bolted upright an uncouth barbarian by the name of CARSON, by former occupation an overseer, and newly promoted by testamentary benevolence to the proud position of a cotton planter.

"Mr. Chairman," he screamed, "I move that Mr. Tharin be required to make no such allusions, but to defend himself from *charges* made against him, and in the briefest manner possible."

"That's so!" "That's it!" traveled from lip to lip around the room, and echoed from many of the crowd without, until the president, rapping with his knuckles, obtained (what *he* called) "order," and, smiling sarcastically, sneered:

"Friends, we are here to listen to a speech from the 'orator of the day' (laughter). One at a time if you please (laughter). You put the culprit (!) on his guard by these unseasonable interruptions.

10*

Besides we—all of us—*are here as members of the
vigilance committee;* therefore his polluting and
anti-southern doctrines can demoralize (!) none of
us. I feel great curiosity to hear him through."

" As I was saying, sir, when interrupted, I have
lived to see secret associations usurp the functions
of the outraged law, and mobs imprison and *even
execute innocent* persons without a trial, judge, or
jury! Alas! I have lived to see the day—"

" You wouldn't live to see many more if I had
the will of you," growled Carson.

" When all the dearest privileges and time-
honored rights of Americans are practically denied; when 'taxation without representation'
oppresses God's poor, for the benefit of the rich,
in every State in this Union, and the non-slaveholders of my native section, although a very
large majority of the population, are compelled
to pay their tribute into the treasury for the benefit of the cotton planters, who monopolize as,
jure divino, their own, all the offices, honors,
and emoluments of government, in direct violation of the very *first* section of the very *first* Article of the Constitution of Alabama." *

---

* " ARTICLE I.—*Declaration of Rights.* (Constitution of
Alabama.)

" That the general, great, and *essential* principles of *liberty*
and free government may be recognized and established, we
declare :

" SEC. 1. That *all* freemen, when they form a social com
pact, are *equal in rights;* and that no man, *or set of men* are

"All *white* men in Alabama are declared *unalterably* free and *equal*. But, under the name of Secession, a Reign of Terror has already overturned the *equality* of white men, and is rapidly degrading, below the level of the negro, every free-born voter who prefers not Secession before his chief joy. Where *now* are *democratical* institutions? Where now is the Democratic Party? Riven in twain,—powerless to save the Union, or even itself,—trampled into dust and mockery! On its ashes *Aristocracy* has reared a *throne*, upon whose downy summit reclines a *despot* whom *I* am commanded to obey as *my* sovereign! 'King Cotton' is his terrible name. He flourishes his bloody sceptre over the 'poor white trash' who encumber the soil sacred to the patent leathers of the 'patriarchs' of the 'peculiar institution.' "

"Why, Dunklin, he's a damned Abolitionist," exclaimed Carson, who could not contain himself another minute.

"Hush, Carson," hissed the irate president through his clenched teeth, at the same time rolling his basilisk eyes askance at the speaker.

"If I speak at all, Mr. Chairman, I will speak as a free white citizen of Alabama should speak. I am coerced into speaking thus by my solemn

---

entitled to exclusive, separate public emoluments or privileges, but in consideration of public services."—*Constitution of Alabama.*

oath. It was to speak I came hither, and to an
audience of my fellow-citizens, *as such!* I came
to say that this land, redeemed by oceans of blood
—some of it the blood of my own ancestry—from
the thralldom of King George III., is now reduced, by means of the gradual encroachments of
that aristocratic class to which you, sirs, affect to
belong, to one grand empire, the monopolist and
monarch of which is 'King Cotton.' It has come
to pass that, in the nineteenth century, a mania,
more engrossing and more unsubstantial than the
'tulip mania' of Holland, has obfuscated the in-
tellects of the people, who can derive no possible
advantage from the coronation of Cotton. Your
secret leagues and orders of modern knight-errantry
have murdered our mother Liberty. Not content
with this, you have rolled to the door of her sepul-
chre a huge cotton bale, and sealed it with your
king's tarry signet. Still unsatisfied, you have
'set a watch'—*Committees of Vigilance*—to guard
the tomb, lest some heaven-inspired resurrectionist
should approach and roll the barrier away!

"The crime for which I was this day to have
been arraigned before an illegal tribunal, is my
attempt to restore my down-trodden fellow-citizens of Alabama to their just *rights*. Born a
freeman, I shall ever remain a freeman! I come
not here to *answer*, but to *make* charges—grave
charges—which should bring the blush of shame
and contrition, not of anger and revenge, to your
cheeks.

"*I* charge *you*, Vigilance Committee, with trampling upon law and liberty; *I* charge *you* with utter disregard of the very first section of the very first article of the Constitution of Alabama;* I charge you with violating all the most sacred provisions of the Constitutions of your own State and of the United States,† and even of your so-called 'Confederate States.' Your very corporate or organic existence is an infraction of, and an insult to, all the principles of the common and the statute law, a mockery of all constitutional stipulations and guarantees, *a usurpation of universal empire*, and a warning to all thinking men of the tendencies of this unnecessary revolution!

"I do not believe that the *whole* membership of this committee is chargeable with a *willful* design to inaugurate a 'reign of terror' in Alabama. This would be too dreadful a charge upon human nature. I think that many of you have been be-

---

* See note on page 114.

† "The right of the people to be secure in their persons, houses, papers, and effects against unreasonable searches and seizures shall not be violated," etc.—*Const. of U. S., Amendments*, Art. VI.

"In all criminal prosecutions the accused shall enjoy the right to a speedy and public trial, by an *impartial jury* of the State and district wherein the crime shall have been committed, which district shall have been previously ascertained by law, and to be informed of the nature and cause of the accusation; to be confronted with the witnesses against him; to have compulsory process for obtaining witnesses in his favor; and to have the assistance of counsel for his defence." —*Const. of U. S., Amendments*, Art. VI.

trayed by your passions, and the excitements of
the hour, into lending yourselves to a movement
fraught with dangers to the State, of which you
took no cognizance in the hurry and turmoil of
the times. I do not believe now that you will attempt to carry out any infamous measure upon
myself. *I am a native of the Southern portion of
these United States* (sensation), and you had better
beware, if such be your intention, lest, in harming
me, you show your enmity to '*Southern Rights*'
(sensation), of which you constitute yourselves
the 'peculiar' guardians. I have friends in Alabama and South Carolina who will avenge my
fall by the utter abolition of the illegal tribunals
which now burden the country with their diabolical and unconstitutional oppressions, and who
will call to a strict account the human instru-
mentalities through whom 'King Cotton' conducts
his despotic usurpations. The people of the South,
although *now* unprepared to see in me their best
friend, will one day do justice to my patriotism,
while that 'small but artful and enterprising minority,'* the cotton planters of the South, will
receive the execrations of civilized mankind!

---

* "All obstructions to the execution of the laws, all *combi-
nations and associations*, under whatever plausible character,
with the real design to direct, control, counteract, or awe the
regular deliberation and action of the constituted authorities,
are destructive of this fundamental principle (loyalty) and of
fatal tendency. They serve to *organize faction*, to give it an
artificial and extraordinary force, to put in place of the dele-

"I have only to demand, in conclusion, that, for the sake of public justice, and, in order to give a citizen his right of self-justification, you abstain from all manifestations of mobocracy toward my person, and that you obtain a warrant for my arrest from the proper legal authority, containing specific charges,—if there be any, really,—with a notice of time and place of trial, by a legally impaneled and sworn jury of my peers.

"This right I claim, together with the right to retire, at once, to my present abode, unmolested and undetained."

The "orator of the day" then sat down, while a deathlike silence pervaded the apartment. His excited vision traveled resolutely—if not calmly—over that throng, noting the effect of his remarks, and weighing his chances of escape. No word being spoken, he rose, took his books from the bench, and, taking his hat in his hand, looked toward his uncle, who, sitting with bent head, seemed frozen to apprehensive silence. Touching him upon the shoulder, he ejaculated, "Come!"

As the two were proceeding toward the door, one of the banditti, Col. ROBERT RIVES, rose, and, in a voice almost inarticulate with passion, moved that the vigilance committee "now go into *secret*

---

gated will of the nation the will of a party, often a *small but artful and enterprising minority* of the community," etc.— *Farewell Address of George Washington,* 17th *September,* 1796.

session."*   As the nephew, with his uncle, was
departing, he heard the question seconded, put,
and carried.   Here was palpable proof of deception and design.   The settled purpose of many of
them was traceable in their tones, which were
"still as the breeze, but dreadful as the storm."

---

* This was contrary to promise, of course, but the whole
course of Rives, from beginning to end, was characterized with
a fell and rabid spirit of destruction.   He was eager to procure
my murder, guilty or not guilty.   He had already made up
his mind, and regarded no pledges or promises whatever

SCENE THE FOURTH.

THE MOB.

"Ah! can you bear contempt? the venomed tongue
Of those, whom ruin pleases? the keen sneer,
The rude reproaches of the rascal herd,—
Who, for the self-same actions, if successful,
Would be as grossly lavish in your praise?"

THOMPSON.

"They praise and they admire they know not what,
And know not whom, but as one leads the other;
And what delight to be, by *such*, extolled,
To live upon *their* tongues and be *their* talk,
Of whom to be dispraised, were no small praise?"

MILTON.

"The good old rule
Sufficeth them, the simple plan,
That they should take, *who have the power*,
And they should keep, *who can*."

SCOTT.

AT the door and front yard of my uncle's humble abode, we found assembled the whole household, who welcomed us back with joy. To their congratulations Uncle Daniel responded in tones of encouragement. My mother wept for joy upon my shoulder. My cousins, with whom "Cousin Robert" was no slight favorite, clasped my hands and rejoiced over me. In the vicinity of this touching scene, my aunt and uncle talked in low

11

tones, while Tenah, the mulatto servant, and constant attendant of my mother, retreated kitchenward, muttering, "I wonder wha' Mass. Robert been do to gib de wite folks so much trouble."

I could not find it in my heart to lessen the brightness of that hour by a single desponding syllable; but the cloud, that overhung my spirit, flung its shadow on my brow. The magnetic effect of that secret session thrilled me with instinctive prescience. I *knew* my reprieve was not a permanent release; but a mere lull in the storm which was even then collecting its electricity for another and more formidable outburst.

The next day was one of unusual quiet at Collirene. The male inhabitants were at a muster in Benton, where Col. Rives, arrayed in his military trappings, I afterward learned, rendered himself very conspicuous in his efforts to get a mob to visit me forthwith; but he was dissuaded by Williams for the present, as the culprit (!) had already appealed to law. So they repaired to a justice of the peace, who to their excited complaints made the following answers in substance, which ought to be kept in everlasting remembrance as an evidence of the "chivalry" of perjury:

1. The culprit could not be found guilty of any crime according to law.

2. He had rightly construed the spirit and letter of the law, which contains no language to describe his acts and intentions, except to justify them.

3. The vigilance committee, therefore, could not act, but the people (meaning *some* people, I suppose, in sufficient numbers) could visit him in such a way as to render the punishment of their acts light upon each, on account of the responsibility of all.

4. The justice of the *peace*, who was sworn to support the State *laws*,—being a Secessionist, from interest, and by nature a tiger,—after having admitted that the laws were explicitly on the victim's side, *advised* his illegal arrest.

" And Felix willing to show the Jews a favor, left Paul bound."

Of all this I was at the time profoundly ignorant, for I was in an agony of suspense at Collirene.

What to do? Flight would involve me in disgrace, perhaps in death. Every man's hand would be against me, and suspicion would gain boldness from any apparent unwillingness to sustain legal measures. No! I would await, in agonized suspense, the trial of *law*, which I had challenged. This, I felt apprehensive, would never be accorded. I knew the tiger-nature of a mob, which, disappointed of its prey, crouches immediately for another spring at the throat of its selected victim. Should the fiendish leaders of the vigilance committee appeal to *that* tiger propensity by artfully playing upon their prejudices and fears, no power in law could *save*, although should law-abiding times be ever known in Alabama, it might *avenge* me.

On the second day after the scenes just recorded, as I was endeavoring to soothe my spirit with a book, my uncle, pale as death, rushed into the room, exclaiming:

"Robert, I see a body of men approaching from the side of Benton, whose infuriated gestures are suggestive of any thing rather than of safety to yourself. They are on their way toward the new academy, where many others are awaiting them."

"Uncle Daniel, where is your gun?"

"In the back room, leaning up in a corner."

"Loaded?"

"Loaded."

"Have you any extra caps?"

"Yes—here are a few."

"Uncle Daniel, take your stand at your shop and forbid them entering your house. Tell them there will be bloodshed, if violence be attempted."

"Courage, my boy, and hope for the best."

The ladies were at the windows for several minutes watching the signs of the multitude. Speaking their wishes, rather than their belief, they would exclaim excitedly from time to time:

THE AUNT.* "Margaret, they are going away!"

THE MOTHER.† "No, no! they are stationing themselves in the wood to prevent escape—don't you see?"

---

* Mrs. Martha Tharin, wife of Daniel C. Tharin.

† Mrs. Margaret E. Tharin, relict of William C. Tharin, deceased.

The Aunt. "There are *enough* of them—the cowards!"

The Mother. " O my God! save my poor boy!"

That prayer was heard!

" Take heart, mother—let me know when they are coming," I said, and stationed myself in a corner, gun in hand, in terrible expectation. Nor had I long to wait. A " committee" of about *twenty-five* was dispatched to " bring the culprit, dead or alive, into the presence of" the mob.

A shriek from the women and children, and a tumult without, drew me toward a chink between the logs, whence, unperceived, I peeped out upon a wild and exciting scene.

Right in their path stood my uncle, who warned the fiends against approaching his premises with violent intent, as there would, in such a case, be bloodshed. But on, on they swept, brandishing their revolvers and unsheathed knives, swearing windy, but not meaningless oaths, as to their determination to " take the traitor, dead or alive;" while a bloodhound, which they had brought to render retreat impossible, barked and gamboled in demoniac delight, anxious for some victim upon whom to exert his sanguinary instinct.

Daniel Tharin now showed himself, every inch, a *man*. Throwing himself before the assassins, by every possible exertion, he endeavored to dissuade or frighten them from their diabolical and unlawful designs.

11*

But not long did they parley at the door, which soon gave way beneath reiterated blows—the shrieks of the women and children arising in wild accompaniment to the ferocious onslaughts.

Then ensued a scene which beggars description. Those two heroic daughters of South Carolina, the mother and the aunt of the imperiled Unionist, re-enacted the celebrated deeds of their renowned *Union* mothers of 1776. They placed themselves before the door of the apartment in which the son and nephew was awaiting certain death—with the excusable resolution, however, *not to die alone;* they denied the right of way to the monsters before them, unless their fangs should first drink their blood! The voice of the mother, in tones of mingled reproach and intercession, the rebukes and withering denunciations of the aunt, the unhesitating manly warnings of the uncle, the cries of the children,—these, interwoven with the bloodthirsty shouts of the frenzied "committee," produced an appalling medley, which was any thing but intelligible to the ears of the only silent individual on the premises.

In the midst of the confusion, the little cousin of the "culprit," Sallie Tharin, entered the room wherein "cousin Robert" was awaiting his fate. She heard him breathe the words, "O God! take care of my family! Lord Jesus, receive my spirit!" This completely overcame the sweet child, and she commenced weeping and wringing her hands. This recalled me to myself, and, turning to her, I said, with such calmness as I could command,

"Sallie dear, you had better retire, and take all the children out of the line of my fire; for this gun will discharge its contents in that direction"— pointing toward the door. "Take the children with you, and get your mother and mine, and the rest, to leave the doorway as soon as the ruffians enter; for I'll kill as many as possible, and this gun will scatter."

It was a double-barreled fowling-piece, one barrel of which was loaded with buck and the other with duck shot.

Controlling her emotion, the child retired, and was making the arrangements, I verily believe, when the voice of Williams, raised to its highest pitch, and evidently intended for me, reached my ears :

"Mrs. Tharin, we intend no violence to your son ; we *only* want to afford him *that trial he demanded day before yesterday.*"

This *trick*—for it proved to be nothing better— succeeded. Uncocking the gun, I leaned it carefully up in the corner, and, to the astonishment of all, advanced into their tumultuous midst, and exclaimed—while my aunt struck up a revolver which was aimed at my head—" *I again appeal to the law! I demand a legal trial!*" *

---

* No person unlawfully arrested, North or South, should omit to demand, before witnesses, a legal trial.

Several revolvers were leveled at the prisoner,
who said, with folded arms—

"Fire away, *gentlemen!* I am an *unarmed* prisoner, entirely at your mercy. *You* are numerous
and well armed—I am single-handed and weaponless. If you are cowardly enough to fire now—
'it is allotted to all men *once* to die.'"

They now commenced dragging me away, when
my mother rushed forward to embrace me. She
was restrained by the brutal crowd. I saw it all,
and, by a sudden force, hurling Williams to the
right and Rives to the left, sprang to her side,
and caught her to my breast, exclaiming—

"I *will* embrace my mother. Mother, if I see
you on earth no more, I beg you to remember I
die a victim to *my patriotism!*"

"And for your father's principles," groaned the
mother.

Some of the crowd had dashed forward, with
ready weapons, to prevent that embrace—perhaps
the last on earth of the mother and her first-born;
but the majesty of Nature restrained their hands,
and in confusion they turned away, while their
victim handed his fainting mother to his aunt,
who was sobbing in the wildest emotion near by.

This, dear mother, perhaps was our last embrace;* but what cares Secession for the dearest

---

* The last time the Unionist heard from his only surviving
parent, he was at Cincinnati, an exile from his native South.
Her letter was dated March 31st, 1861. Whether it will ever
again be permitted them to look on each other in this world

of human ties? The man who would *violently* sunder this glorious Union, would ruthlessly trample upon *all* humanities, and even mock at God! The man who would fight in battle for *any* other purpose than to restore it, is a murderer!

---

of storm, is a subject for conjecture only. An extract here may not be quite out of place. It will illustrate the plans of the vigilance committee, and the manner in which they finish up the work they once undertake—hesitating at no falsehoods to sustain their "party," as Mrs. Tharin shrewdly suggests:

"Robert Rives, who appears to be very busy in saying any thing that has a tendency to save his party, told your uncle Daniel that he heard that you were writing and speaking on the horrors of slavery. I, for one, cannot, neither will I, believe such a report; but misrepresentation and misunderstanding have caused much real sorrow to us already. Yes! I assure you that after you left, the anguish I felt is indescribable. I thought I should have died. I could neither eat nor sleep. When I received your letter, and found that you, my dear persecuted child, were safe and well, and among friends, I felt most grateful to kind Providence for guiding you safely from cruel foes and a bitter-hearted set of men, who have not God before their eyes. If there is any justice in *law*, it is my desire and request to you, that you will not suffer these men to go unpunished. You can make every one of them suffer for their unlawful seizure and detention of you. You must vindicate your character, as it is and ought to be dear to us all." (Dear mother, am I not *now* and *here* vindicating my character? I hope this may reach your eye—even if its writer never more behold your venerated face.) "You have friends sufficient to help you in the case, and who, I feel satisfied, will do so. *This* case is one in a thousand. Persons all around here are crying shame upon such unlawful and mean conduct.

"Your aunt Martha and myself were sitting in the room the other day, sewing, when two gentlemen of very respectable

The children, led by their father, now pressed forward to kiss "Cousin Robert," and, after the touching parting, I said, smiling sadly—
" Don't be frightened, little ones: I'll be back soon. The *law* will vindicate my innocence.— Now, sirs, I am ready for trial!"

---

appearance rode up to the gate, and, after bowing very respectfully, asked us if this was Mr. D. C. Tharin's house that was broken open to get at Mr. R. S. Tharin? We told them it was. They then asked ' if we knew any of their names.' Martha called some names, which they took down in their pocketbook." .... " We do not know who these gentlemen can be. They said something about Wetumpka, whither they were going, or where they had been, I can't say which, but they mentioned Wetumpka."

Again she writes in the same letter : " I really think this piece of business is already stirring ; therefore, my dear son, I think it advisable that you should remain *quiet*. Write or say *nothing at all* on the *subject* of slavery, as you may again be misrepresented. Brother Edward wrote (from Charleston, S. C.) to brother Daniel, inclosing a piece, which he cut from a paper, which states that you intended publishing an Abolition paper, to be called the *Non-slaveholder*—leaving out, to suit its own views, that it was to have been published at *Montgomery*, as the editor knew a paper published in a *Southern* city *could not be* one of that sort. The piece Edward sent to Daniel, said the above was communicated by *Robert Rives.* I have no faith in that man. *They are all trembling for* FEAR. Therefore I say again, be cautious. The piece I allude to says also that ' the punishment, though physically slight, was degrading.' Edward also inclosed to Daniel another piece. Both of the pieces are headed, ' ORDERED OFF,' &c."

As a proper comment on this letter, I will here add the 27th section of Art. I. of Alabama's Constitution (Bill of Rights) :

" Emigration from this State shall not be prohibited, nor shall any citizen *be exiled*."—Art. I., § 27.

"Trial—Hell!" shouted an infuriated mobocrat; "you've had your trial, and now you will suffer your punishment!"

"Hold that dog!" cried a voice; "or he'll render a trial a useless formality."

"Down! down, sir!" commanded the hound's owner, at the same time grasping him by the collar and calling for assistance. The dog had eyed the prisoner, as if to make sure that he was the object of all this hubbub, and, having seen the frantic movements of those who were dragging him along, had crouched for a spring at his throat, when the intervention of Williams prevented a catastrophe.

As the guard and their prisoner approached the " *new** academy," a barbaric scene burst upon their view. About two hundred and fifty planters, great and small (many of whom claimed to belong to the first families), and their sycophants, are congregated around the building, awaiting in various attitudes and occupations the return of their messengers. As the latter approach, a voice, from the midst of the expecting crowd, demands—

"Have you got the d—d rascal?"

"Got him! I reckon we have."

A shout ascends from the assembly, who, from their recumbent or oblique attitudes, start into bustling activity. Some replenish their mouths with new supplies of tobacco; some ignite fresh

---

* It will be remembered that the vigilance committee had met in the *old* academy.

cigars, or throw away old ones; some fire their pistols in the air; some rush into the building, and some apply themselves to their whisky bottles, with hilarious enjoyment.

Carson, who had been quite demonstrative, waiting until the prisoner drew near enough to be seen and recognized, exclaimed—

"Tharin, see how *popular* you are, and how we rejoice at your advent!"

"Good! Good! Bully for you, Carson; try it again!" shouted the crowd.

The "prisoner," "traitor," "rascal," or "culprit," as I was variously denominated, being conducted into the house, the others tumultuously followed, and took the seats which ought to have remained sacred to Education and Liberty, but which were now prostituted to the unhallowed and murderous designs of the ringleaders of that tiger-mob.

"I move," said Williams, "that this meeting appoint Dr. Dunklin our president."

"Second the motion," said a voice.

Upon taking his seat, the chairman thanked the meeting for the distinguished honor it had done him in appointing him to preside over so intelligent and patriotic a body. He would have preferred that some more distinguished gentleman had been elevated to the honorable but responsible duty of presiding over their deliberations. The great events that were daily transpiring in the South would soon be read in Europe, and bring down the applause of kings and princes. Among the most dangerous enemies of the South were those who, in her very midst, grew dissatisfied with her peculiar and patriarchal institutions, and, of course, *with the rule of those who advocated and upheld their extension.* These men were the more hateful because they considered King Cotton a despot, and his followers, rebels. The misguided young man who was to be arraigned that day before the majestic tribunal of public opinion, merited public vengeance, and would doubtless receive it."

Amid great applause, the "honors" were shared with a secretary, "Professor" Harris, of Virginia, the teacher who daily presided over that very academy; and the meeting was formally declared ready for the transaction of business.

A lawyer of Monterey, Alabama, named Powell, who, like the prisoner, *had sworn,* when admitted to practice law in the courts of the State, to "support the Constitution of the United States and the Constitution of Alabama, and never, for considerations personal to himself, to neglect the cause of the defenseless and oppressed," demanded of the committee, "whether Mr. Tharin had come *willingly,* or *unwillingly,* with his captors."

Mr. Williams answered, that the prisoner certainly gave himself up, but that it was very unwillingly indeed; and that he believed the prisoner was still dissatisfied with the course of the

12

people (!),* and that his mother had denominated the committee *a brutal mob*."

"The prisoner" here rose and asked Mr. Williams if I did not surrender myself in consequence of Mr. Williams' own promise *that I should have a legal trial, and immediately on receiving that assurance.*

This produced great commotion. Some person shouted, "Shut up, damn you!" The president called "order," and Williams sat down; while Powell, anxious to increase the excitement, and raging with ebullient fury, demanded of Williams whether the prisoner had not behaved *insolently* to the committee.

"Rather so," admitted Williams.

POWELL. "How did Old-man Tharin behave?"

WILLIAMS. "I regret to say that Mr. Daniel Tharin being unwilling that the committee should enter his house, we had to do so by force."

THE PRISONER. "It was natural for my uncle to be excited, under the circumstances. As he acted according to my own suggestions, I hope no one save myself will be held responsible for *my* acts. *I* am not ashamed of them."

THE PRESIDENT (*savagely*). "Silence, Mr. Tharin! You will find it dangerous to interrupt these proceedings again!"

The applause that greeted this unparliamentary

---

* I beg the reader to discriminate between *the* people and *some* people.

act was absolutely deafening. The prisoner sat down, and almost gave up all for lost.

This desultory discussion was intended to work up the passions of the illiterate mob to the highest pitch, and continued so long as to involve great peril to the prisoner. At length, some one,* premising that "since Mr. Tharin had demanded a legal trial, and since the justice of the peace at Benton had told the committee, who had been appointed to see him yesterday, '*that warrants were not issuable for the offense*† *committed by Mr. Tharin, or supposed to have been committed by him*,' and since we cannot wait for the *slow proceedings of court-house machinery*,‡—he suggested, therefore, that a jury of twelve should proceed to try Mr. Tharin, *then and there*, and that the meeting pledge itself to abide by its verdict"—which motion, without division or repetition, was vociferously carried.

By another vote, the chair was authorized to nominate the "jury," *who were not to be sworn*, when the miserable caricature of justice commenced, the president, I suppose, being the *judge*,

---

* I was not in a situation to ask for names.

† "The people shall be *secure* in their *persons*, houses, papers, and possessions, from unreasonable seizures or searches; and no warrant to search any place, or *seize any person* or thing, shall issue, without describing them as nearly as may be, nor without probable cause, supported by oath or affirmation."— *Constitution of Alabama*, Art. I., sec. 9.

‡ The *general* excuse all over the whole country for arbitrary arrests.

but the prisoner being refused the privilege of challenging a single *juror*,—if a man not bound by *oath* can be considered a *juror*,—and the prisoner, on motion of the chivalrous Carson, being also denied any speech before the "jury." *

The prisoner demanded time to summon witnesses from Wetumpka, and procure other testimony. But this was, of course, refused. *

" May I ask one favor, Mr. President ?" respectfully demanded the prisoner.

PRESIDENT. " Well! what do you want ?"

" I want Mr. Powell, who is a lawyer, *sworn, like myself, to support the Constitutions of this* State, and of the United States, and who also, like myself, recorded his oath, when admitted to practice law, that ' *never*, for considerations personal to himself, would he neglect the cause of the defenseless and oppressed'—to defend *my* cause before this 'jury.' "

" Really, Mr. Tharin," said Powell, " I start for home immediately, as I have business there."

---

* " In all criminal prosecutions, the accused has a right to be heard by himself and counsel ; to demand the nature and cause of the accusation, and have a copy thereof ; to be confronted with the witnesses against him ; to have compulsory process for obtaining witnesses in his favor, and, in all prosecutions by indictment, or information, a speedy public trial by an impartial jury of the county, or district, in which the offense shall have been committed ; he shall not be compelled to give evidence against himself, nor shall he be deprived of his life, *liberty*, or property, but by *due course of law*."—*Const. Ala.*, Art. I., § 10.

Saying this, he left the apartment, but, returning, five minutes afterward, took the side of the *prosecution*, and was peculiarly unlawyerlike and violent from beginning to end.

What a demon is the spirit of Radicalism! whose votaries *perjure* themselves willingly, *even proudly*, whenever their oaths to support *their own State Constitutions*, or the national Constitution itself come in conflict with their interests or passions! "State *rights!*" "individual *rights!*" Republicanism! — away with the hypocritical cant of Treason. The non-slaveholders—the *people* North and South, who love the Union more than sectionalism,—might well exclaim:

" We've had *wrongs* to stir a fever in the blood of age, and make the infant's sinews strong as steel!"

There is not a single sworn lawyer or official North or South, who sustains the right of Radicals to mob, punish, or arrest Unionists, to rob the public treasury, to suppress free speech, or to indulge in *any* unconstitutionalities whatever, who is not a perjurer before God, and deserving of the reprobation of all *honest* men!

Powell but imitated, on a small scale, the leaders of Secession in his own State and elsewhere, and deserves no more reprobation, *and no less*, than the Yanceys, the Rhetts, the Davises, the Stephenses, the Floyds, the Masons and Slidells, *et id omne genus*, whose opportunities, or talents, afford them a wider field for the display of their villainy!

The right of Secession, as it is called, even if it exist in a State, separately, and without the consent of all her co-States, to dissolve the Union, can not, even in the opinion of its warmest advocate,—if he be a *gentleman*, not to say *patriot*, which no Radical can be considered,—legalize robbery, false imprisonment, perjury, *unlawful duress*, murder, exile, libel, and slander. A man may possibly arrive at an honest conviction that this or that State, or even section is wronged, but *two wrongs not making a right*,—still it becomes him to express himself without mendacity, and to conduct himself without dishonor and dishonesty.

Political honesty had become so unfashionable in Alabama, that I was about to suffer for being true to my oath, and to my own convictions of duty under that oath.

Villains seize the darkness of midnight for the perpetration of their rascalities.

Political villains had seized upon the darkness produced by their own diabolisms, to aim the assassin's dagger at the heart of political honesty and truth. Rioting in the licentiousness of the mob they had engendered, they fattened, like blow-flies, upon the garbage which is their natural element.

Like all noxious vermin, they should have been gotten rid of before the body politic became infested with their presence, and all its members grew rotten with the ulceration of their incisive attacks.

Had President Buchanan possessed either honesty or courage, this necessary cautery would have been practiced.

Powell being the only—at least, the most noisy —lawyer in the mob, managed to browbeat " the prisoner" into a submission, which he could never have obtained, if, man to man, we had met. But as the crowd of Radicals silenced me whenever I attempted to speak, and encouraged Powell, it was very easy to establish the following facts :*

1. I had *conversed* with several *non*-slaveholders in the neighborhood on the subject of *their* Southern Rights!

2. I was about to establish, at Montgomery, a newspaper to be called *The Non-slaveholder.*

3. I was organizing the people into secret associations, for the *repeal, by convention,* of the Ordinance of Secession.

But the malignity of the mob was not satisfied with these *facts*, not one of which was denied by their victim. The measure of their iniquitous proceedings could not be full, until they had dragged in the " everlasting nigger." Otherwise, incompleteness would be stamped upon their meeting, and even reaction might ensue, honorable to the captive and dangerous to themselves.

Radicalism in both sections feeds upon only one idea—*nigger.* Take the *nigger* out of the dumpling, and Radicalism dies for want of appetite.

---

* Vide pp. 144–152, inclusive.

In spite, therefore, of the palpable absurdity of supposing that the Secret Union Association was an *Abolition* movement, or that the "*Non-slave-holder*," to be published at *Montgomery*, was to have been an open advocate of *Abolition*, these things were charged upon the Unionist, because thus alone could they get rid of him and his Conservative doctrines on the great national question of Union or Disunion.

The *charge* of being an Abolitionist was, therefore, inevitable. *Proofs* were not absolutely necessary—the *name itself* was enough for any Southern mob to grow wild on.

A witness, previously suborned, viz., the same John V. Buford, or Beaufort, who had impeached him before the vigilance committee, was introduced. Powell led the witness to the declaration that Tharin was a "rank Abolitionist," because he had heard the latter say he wanted to "abolish *monopolies*," and that that *must have meant* slavery, in his (Beaufort's) opinion.

PRISONER. "May I not ask the witness one question?"

Much discussion ensued as to whether this poor privilege should be granted, and finally it was accorded with a very bad grace.

PRISONER. "Mr. Beaufort."

The witness, who had risen respectfully to answer Powell, obstinately retained his seat.

PRISONER (fixing his eye firmly on the witness). "Mr. Beaufort!"

No better result.

PRISONER (with a stamp of his foot). " Witness ! *rise* when I speak to you !"

Poor Beaufort was absolutely galvanized to his feet. Trembling all over, and pale as death, he gasped, with blanched lips and husky throat—

" Sir !"

" Beaufort, don't answer the d—d traitor," shouted Powell, who was joined by many others with loud shouts, oaths, and threatening gestures.

The " traitor," as *they* called the loyal man, still kept his eye upon Beaufort, who had sat down, overwhelmed with shame and the stings of a guilty conscience.

" Mr. Tharin, do not intimidate the witness," bawled the inevitable Carson.

" Do not be *alarmed*, Mr. Beaufort; I shall ask you no question. Your *manner* can not fail to convince any one of common sense that you have told nothing but lies !"

Here the confusion became terrific. Some " gritted" their teeth, others cursed and swore ; but others still seemed disposed to disbelieve Beaufort, exclaiming — " Very strange !" One man made bold to say—

" Why, John Beaufort looks a d—d sight more guilty than Tharin !"

Seizing upon this opportunity, the beleaguered man sprang to his feet, and exclaimed—

" Fellow-citizens, judge, yourselves, between us ! Here is a man larger than I, who trembles at my glance, although he has two hundred and fifty armed men to back him. If you take his evidence against me after that, it is *because you thirst for my blood!*"

A witness was admitted to the stand, who testified that Mr. Tharin had met him on the road, asked him if he had any negroes, received an affirmative reply, and remarked to him that he had better sell them quickly, because that kind of property was valueless in civil war, and that Abolition and Secession were identical in their effects.

One of the " poor white trash," who had agreed to subscribe to the *Non-slaveholder,* was made to testify, much to the amusement of the crowd, in opposition to his own views and feelings :

POWELL (quietly). " Mr. Eddings, were you ever down at Monterey?"

EDDINGS (nervously). " Monterey! — Do you mean Monterey in Mexico?"

POWELL (sarcastically). " No! Monterey in Alabama."

EDDINGS (blandly). " Well, yes!"

POWELL (courteously). " Have you any objection to say why you left Monterey?"

EDDINGS (excitedly). " That's my business!"

POWELL (coolly). " Did you ever know of a man named Powell down there?"

EDDINGS (alarmed). " Mr. Powell, I thought you wanted me here as a witness in *this* trial!"

POWELL (insinuatingly). " So we do! *and if*

*you'll testify right in this trial, I'll say no more
about that other matter.*"

EDDINGS (brightening). " Oh ! certainly !"

POWELL. " Now, Mr. Eddings, do you not understand *non*-slaveholder to mean—*Abolitionist?*"

EDDINGS. " Now you speak of it, I begin to see
it in that light."

POWELL. " Did not Tharin tell you his paper
would destroy slavery ?"

EDDINGS. " Yes—slavery of *white* people."

POWELL (peremptorily). " Answer my questions
as I ask them. Do you think Mr. Tharin cares a
damn for the institution of slavery ?"

EDDINGS. "No—not for *them that own it.*"

POWELL. " Would you like to go to Monterey
with me ?"

EDDINGS (alarmed). " Good God ! no ! sir."

POWELL. " Does Tharin care a damn for the institution of slavery ?"

EDDINGS. " No sir-ree !"

Here the crowd commenced cheering Powell,
and, amid much laughter, prepared themselves for
the next funny scene.

THE SECRETARY (Prof. Harris) testified that Mr.
Tharin had told him he did not care a cent for *any*
" peculiar" institution.

" Big Dudley," a young cotton-planter, a frantic Secessionist, a member of that dignified body,—
the unsworn jury of twelve,—objected to the admission of " old man Tharin on the stand ; because," he said, " old Tharin (had) *behaved scan-*

dalous in not admitting them into his house, without making such a d—d fuss about it."

But, at length, after much stupid opposition, the prisoner's uncle was admitted as a witness, mainly because he was *a member of the same church* with some of the "*jury.*"

Daniel Tharin testified to facts diametrically at variance with the testimony of the crest-fallen Beaufort, who was so completely disconcerted that he did not even raise his eyes, and, when the cross-examination was over, hope began to return to the prisoner's heart.

The sketch, which has just been given, of that long trial, is short, in comparison, it is true; but, from its commencement to its conclusion, it occupied nearly nine hours of keen suspense to the captive, but of keen enjoyment to his persecutors. As soon as the "testimony" was concluded, at about 7 P. M., it was moved that the "audience" retire, while the "jury," in secret session, should consult as to their verdict.

A committee of three was appointed to guard the prisoner, and the "jury" was left alone with the president of the meeting.

SCENE THE FIFTH.

THE VERDICT.

"What can innocence hope for,
When such as sit her judges are corrupt?"
                                    MASSINGER.

"Man is unjust; but God is just, and finally justice tri-
umphs."   LONGFELLOW.

As soon as the recess was known in the village,
trays, filled with coffee and eatables, approached
upon the heads of female slaves, with the compliments of "missis," to refresh the *gentlemen* after
their *patriotic* labors.

I swallowed some coffee, but abstained from
eating. Although I felt my life hung upon a
single thread, I perceived that thread to be *presence of mind! That* lost, *I* was lost. I found
that many of the mob were departing, and that
those who remained were worn out with the
tedium of the trial. I perceived that my only
hope of saving my life (should the "verdict" of
the "jury" demand it) was, by at once creating
a reaction in the minds of the bystanders. I
commenced by praising the coffee, complained
of the cramped condition of my limbs, after sit-

ting so long in one position, proposed a short walk to the committee, which was willingly agreed to, and joined in the conversation with my guard, until their interest was excited against their will.

I told them how I loved the whole nation,— North, South, East, and West,—too much to see with pleasure the severance of a Union, that Washington had described as the "palladium of our safety;" that, when war too soon should drench the land with kindred blood, and when each family was mourning some loved and lost one,—when the full consequences of Secession were upon the State of Alabama, they *would* know, what now they were determined to ignore, that

"THE UNION IS THE PALLADIUM OF THEIR SAFETY!"

I had not ceased talking when we returned to the mob, and I had won the committee, or guard, to a better understanding of my views and feelings. One by one the crowd gradually collected around us, and listened to the conversation. One of the Dudleys said he believed that Mr. Tharin was in correspondence with Northern Abolition societies. The prisoner stated that, situated as he then was, he could not resent this intended insult; but that he never saw or communicated with Abolitionists in his life, and that the charge originated in either a culpable mistake, or else in the unscrupulous misrepresentations of his Disunion calumniators, who hesitated at no means to de-

stroy a man whose views on the subject of "Union"
were so well defined as his own.

In this way, although my thoughts were necessarily more with the future than with the present,
I sustained a desultory conversation for (what
seemed to me) four or five hours, which, however
tedious, I would willingly have prolonged.

The Southern mind is peculiarly susceptible to
change. It admires courage, and despises the
reverse. We do not acknowledge a consciousness
of fear, and detest those who manifest it. We
respect even our victims who conceal their appre-
hensions. It would be an empty panegyric to say
that the subject of this sketch *felt no fear*, for he
writhed in his inmost soul under the inflictions of
suspense; but, says Shakspeare—

> "The brave man is not he who *feels* no fear,
> For that were foolish and irrational;
> But he whose steadfast soul despises fear,
> And nobly dares the danger nature shrinks from."

The secret session of the "jury" was protracted
to a late hour, and the patience of the outsiders
was taxed to its utmost. At length the doors
were thrown open, and the eager throng resumed
the benches.

A sepulchral silence pervaded the assembly.
The "president" called the meeting to order, and
announced that the jury would read their verdict
through their secretary, "the professor."

With pedantic emphasis, "Professor" Harris
pronounced the following

"VERDICT.

"We, the 'jury,' find the defendant guilty, and decide that his punishment shall be as follows:

"1. He shall receive thirty-nine lashes, *as a disgrace.*

"2. As soon as this shall be concluded, he shall be escorted, by a committee of five, to Benton, and placed in charge of the captain of the first boat which stops there.

"3. *Should he ever return to this community, he shall be hanged.*

"4. The proceedings of this meeting shall be published in the Montgomery *Advertiser* and *Post.*"

A profound hush attended and followed the sonorous enunciation of the sentence. With a calmness that astonished myself no less than my audience, I said:

"This, then, is *your* decision. It would be as unmanly for me to *ask* any commutation of this 'punishment,' as it is unmanly in you to meditate so gross an outrage. But I do not suppose you make war upon defenseless *women and children.* The immediate publication in the papers of your proceedings will probably kill my wife, who, I learn, is very sick; I, *therefore*, move that a postponement of four weeks be granted, for the benefit of persons whom even you acknowledge innocent."

No word was spoken for some time, when a feeble voice said, "I second the motion."

"We don't war on women; but we don't intend you to escape that way. *You wish to escape us;* but you can't, and you shan't!" Thus spoke Rives, who, from the same "jury," was followed by Carson, who thus relieved himself:

"Mr. President, the papers found on this man's person show his statement to be a fact. But I may as well state that his papers also show that he took a case for a William S. Middlebrooks, of Wetumpka, accused of '*Lincolnism!*'"

"I will also state," cried the blood-thirsty Rives, "that five of this 'jury,' myself among the number, voted to hang the traitor, and only gave way because we could not convince the others that death was not too severe a punishment." Then turning to the victim of mobocracy, he exclaimed, at the same time shaking his fist: "We know our rights, and, knowing, *dare* maintain!"

"Considering the disparity of numbers, sir," I retorted, "that is a very cheap declaration. It is my own opinion, there is very little daring in *your* present course. But, Mr. President, I insist on my motion, which has received a second."

Here a Doctor (Somebody) moved that the motion be amended, by inserting *six* instead of *four* weeks, adducing medical reasons to show that ladies are liable to serious injury by any shock to the nervous system under six weeks.

By an overwhelming vote the amendment was lost, *Rives voting in the negative.*

This was his *chivalry!*

13*

The original motion was barely carried, *Rives again voting in the negative.*

It was moved that the chairman appoint a committee of three to carry into effect the first article of the verdict. .

Messrs. Carson, Dudley, and "Big Dudley" (we know not their *Christian* names) were *honored* with the appointment, and proceeded to its discharge with evident trepidation. They were told not to *hurt* the prisoner, but merely to *disgrace* him. Remembering the fable of the "Oak and the Reed," I bowed before the storm I could not resist, in order to rise upright after the storm should have passed. This was all I had left to do. Had I *resisted* those light and harmless blows, which were *intended* only to "disgrace" me, I would have been murdered, weaponless as I was, *in cold blood*. Over my grave would have settled the night of *oblivion*. Calumniators would have detracted from my reputation unchecked, and no one could have defended my memory from their violent attacks. This has been the fate of hundreds, thousands! of Unionists. I submitted to the dreadful ordeal, therefore, because I knew the effects of that outrage would not disgrace *me*, while my enemies were engraving upon *their* souls the red stripes of guilt which "all the drops in Neptune's ocean" could not efface. Sustained by a sense of right,—even proud to receive the "stripes" for my defence of the "stars,"—I could almost see the tearful face of Washington leaning from heaven and bidding me, "in patience possess thou thy soul!" I felt not the blows, I saw not the forms of my persecutors; a sarcastic smile rested on my lip, while a peace of mind, which was as incomprehensible as it was grateful, stole over my interiors. I remembered *who* was scourged, when Pilate yielded his own convictions to the mob of Calvary. The crown of thorns was the earthly portion of my *Saviour*. It is true, that Saviour, being Divine, human cruelty and outrage could not "*disgrace*" him. But Truth, the great sanctifier, sustains the meanest of her disciples, blunts the points of the thorns, heals their undeserved stripes, and, through the conscience, teaches them to defy the terrors of persecution.

After the outrage had been perpetrated, *who*, I ask, was *disgraced?*—the martyr, or the mob?

From a lordly height of mental, political, and conscientious superiority, the victim *looked down* upon his foes. They seemed to have suddenly become dwarfed, in the stature of the inner man, to Liliputian diminutiveness. From the corruption of their thoughts was stripped the vail of opaque flesh. The lava waves of hell were coursing through their arteries. Mercy, Truth, and Peace had fled forever from their dismantled shrines; and Cruelty, Perjury, and Murder chased each other, in diabolical sport, through the corridors of Memory. Thereafter, from worse to worse, the pathways of those mobocrats paralleled into a continuous descent. For them, no more would

shine the sun of Truth. Gross darkness obscured
their vision, and they groped their way to ruin,
seeking their congenial Tartarus, where their law
and their gospel consist in this quintessence of
rebellion—

"*Better* to *rule in hell* than *serve in heaven!*"

A committee of five was next appointed, among
whom were Rush, "Big Dudley," Dr. Carver, and
Jeff. Rives, to carry out the second provision of
the verdict. These were appointed because they
were well mounted, and supplied with superior
revolvers.

It was deemed a matter of importance that an
animal should be procured for the use of the prisoner suited to the purpose. Some time was passed
in preparing a beast—and *such* a beast! A mule,
of medium proportions, whose trick consisted in
stopping whenever he was urged forward.

During the interval, the victim of mobocracy
was allowed to see his mother, who was, however,
so frantic with grief as to be unable to hold
connected conversation. Of a sanguineous tem-
perament, she was naturally excitable, and the
irritating cause was of a magnitude sufficient to
overthrow stronger nerves. Clasping her son to
her bosom, she shrieked rather than said—

"Go to Charleston, my son! go to Charleston! I think your relatives there will protect
you!"

Quick as lightning the thought flashed through
my brain that to appear to acquiesce would mis-

lead my enemies who still meditated my death, and, so, I said:

"Very well! mother, I will go thither. Cheer up, and you will soon hear of my safety."

Then turning to my Aunt Martha, I said:

"If any thing should happen to me, tell my brother to avenge my death, and, in any case, assure him solemnly that I never was and never can be an Abolitionist, that my Unionism is my only offence; that Secession—Radicalism—I hate with a perfect hatred!"

"And well you may!" she replied, bursting into tears.

The solemn leave-taking over, your fellow-citizen, unlawfully captured, unlawfully detained, unlawfully dealt with, and now unlawfully driven into exile, seized his portmanteau, packed by his mother's trembling hands, and mounted his "nondescript animal" for a midnight tramp through roads covered with a thick layer of sticky prairie mud, and under the escort of a set of ruffians, who discharged their pistols, drank whisky, and "patroled for niggers" on the way. Meeting a "nigger" on the road, they asked him for his "pass;" not having any, his whisky jugs were broken, and, being stripped for the purpose, he was laid prostrate on the earth. These preliminaries concluded, with a bridle-rein they whipped him, amid vociferous cheers on the one side and entreaties on the other. I sat my mule like monumental marble, without manifesting either

surprise or indignation. My own sufferings were
too fresh in my mind to permit any outward in-
dication of the thoughts which were busy within
me. I wondered that the Caucasian barbarians,
who " escorted" me, did not recur to the speech I
had made before the vigilance committee in the
old academy, when I had said :

" All *white* men in Alabama were born free and
equal ; but, under the name of Secession, a reign
of terror has already overturned even the nominal
equality of white men, *and is rapidly degrading
to the level of the negro every free-born voter who
prefers not Secession before his chief joy.* On the
ashes of democracy, ' aristocrats' have erected a
throne, upon whose downy summit reclines a despot, whom they call ' King Cotton,' whose invisible hand *flourishes the lash over the heads of
the ' poor white trash'* who encumber the soil,
sacred to the patent-leathers of the patriarchs of
the peculiar institution !"

When our forefathers planned that proud banner, the Stars and Stripes, what fiend from hell
dared to write this invisible sentence on its folds:

" The day shall come, when he who would defend the stars, shall receive the stripes !"

Interwoven with the stars of Independence,
were *and are* the stripes of despotism ! The slaveholder walks with his head among the stars—the
poor non-slaveholder sinks beneath the *glorious
stripes!* The cotton-planter imports every thing
except his negroes from the North, and sends back

in return—whipped freemen. The cotton-planter makes his black slave a bricklayer, or a blacksmith, or a wheelwright, and then insolently asserts that the Yankees alone want *negro equality* in the South. The great champion of the cotton-planters, William L. Yancey, in his "great" speech at Cincinnati, 24th October, 1860, said:

"But *you*, gentlemen, want to place the negro and the white man upon a common level. You do it by appealing to the passions and prejudices of the people. You will get, by this means, *a mulatto government.* And, when you have done this, *what effect will it have on the great mass of free laborers.* Now it moves in a higher sphere,— the sphere of free-labor, the sphere of *freedom*, but, *then, this vast mass of slave labor* will be mixed up with it *so as to come in contact with you daily. They will elbow you on the streets, in the workshops, on the roads, and in the field. They will underbid you for every species of labor*, for they have no wish beyond the satisfaction of to-day."

See what a *home-picture* Mr. Yancey has drawn. *How* did Mr. Yancey *know* that the negroes, if allowed to flood Cincinnati with black mechanics, would come daily in contact with the poor white laborer? How did he know that they would *underbid* him?

Mr. Yancey was drawing a *home-picture!* He had *seen*, all his life, in the cities, and towns, and villages of the South, *the very thing* he described so graphically to a Northern audience. He had

seen the rich man's negro " come in contact" with
the poor white blacksmith, the poor white bricklayer, carpenter, wheelwright, and agriculturist.
He had seen the *preference* invariably given to the
rich man's negro in all such pursuits and trades ;
like me, *he* had heard the *complaints* of the poor
white mechanic of the South against this very
negro equality the rich planters were rapidly
bringing about. These things he had heard and
seen in Charleston, New Orleans, Mobile, Montgomery, and Wetumpka. It was from ocular and
auricular demonstration he spoke, when he exclaimed—

" Are you willing, my hard-handed, hard-working countrymen of the *North*, to be placed on a
level with the black man? Are you willing to
get on the platform prepared for you by this
fanatical party at the North? Do you want to
compete, in your industrial pursuits, with the
black nigger?"

Do *you?* brethren of the South, relatives and
fellow-citizens of the exile who publishes these
lines? Have not the planters for years condemned
every mechanic in the South to negro equality?
Does not Yancey himself confess it? Are my
hard-working, hard-handed fellow-citizens of the
South willing any longer to be placed on a level
with the black man?

Oh! when he asked that question of the mechanics of Cincinnati, how Yancey *sneered!* And
yet, it was a *home-picture.* He thought of *you,*

non-slaveholders of Alabama, and of the South, and, while he thought, he *sneered!*

And yet, how you *cheer* him, when he bids you fight for this *negro equality*, toil for this proud aristocracy, that despises and sneers at, while it uses you. They think all you are fit for is to "turn bullets" for them—*your betters*, who call you "*poor white trash!*"

Degraded America!

Gods! if *one* non-slaveholder, whom I know, could only have his rights to-day in Alabama, I'd stump the dear old State for the Union once more, and leave the *planters*, who stick to treason, to die in the "last ditch," which they so cunningly prepared *for you.*

And you would help me—if you deserve the name of men, if you be worthy of the glorious ancestry from which you sprung—if you be, indeed, superior to the negro, who is now preferred before you! Yes, preferred before you; for, while the rich colonel, or major, who commands a regiment of such men as you by hereditary right, sends his black body-servant sweeping over the field on his gallant steed, you—"poor buckras"— who, owning no negroes, are not exempt, lift your heavy knapsacks to fight for *his* and *his negroes'* interests, *not your own* rights. It is true, some of the understrappers are put to dig your *intrenchments*—but, too often, do they prepare your *graves!*

Cuffy is not permitted to *read;* for *his master*

14

says it unfits him for *submission*. Why do they prevent *you* from reading *this?* If you are reading it now, you are doing so by stealth. You dare not *read* the *truth*, much less *speak* it, while you fight for your independence!

Oh, my down-trodden brethren of the South! will you, too, join in the outcry of my enemies and *your* enemies, who, after they have enslaved *you*, have exiled *your only champion*, because he loves you more than life? The Irish venerate the name of John Mitchell; the Hungarian idolizes his Kossuth—who, when exiled, found in this country a welcome: has the American citizen quite forgotten Washington? Shall it be said that, blinded by the fruitless hope of "*owning a slave some day*," or obfuscated by the aristocratic recollection of having *once* owned one or more, the non-slaveholders of the South *persecute one of their own number*, who dares to reiterate the sentiments of Washington? Remember, it was Washington, whose last public act was to admonish us against disunion: "The Union is the palladium of your *safety!*" Precious legacy to a once free and happy people! When will that people throw off the yoke of bondage, and hail their only safety in a peaceful reunion, in which, the negro slave being confined to the *cotton* field, there will be no more negro equality! Has not the event proved the truth of the prophecy of Washington, when he warned us against party spirit?

One moment of true Southern Rights—*one* day

of freedom to the non-slaveholders of Alabama—
one convention of the *people* who voted for the
Union, and whose votes were not counted, and
the remotest nation of earth would look with
astonishment upon the mighty result!

Some of the class to which I address myself,
although they cannot be ranked among the planters of cotton, taking up the cry of the Charleston
Mercury, are loud in their cheers for Yancey, the
"Garibaldi" of the South. Little do they know
the man they praise. In Cincinnati he proved
himself the enemy of the South, and the trampler
upon "Southern Rights." Only three months and
eighteen days before he advocated, signed, and
rejoiced over the Secession ordinance at Montgomery, on which he opposed giving you and me
a ratification vote—which we never had, of course,
or things would have been different,—only three
months and eighteen days prior to his voice and
vote in the Montgomery Convention, William L.
Yancey said :

"In the Constitution, *they* ordained that the
(U. S.) government was formed for themselves
and *their* posterity ? *Who* were *they?* There was
no slave in that Convention that formed the Constitution. There was no negro there! There were
neither slaves nor negroes in that body that
wrote the Declaration of Independence. But
those men were the representatives of the slaveholding community,—SLAVEHOLDERS THEMSELVES,
who wrote it down *in* the Constitution, that the

Constitution *they* made was for *themselves and their posterity!*"

None but slaveholders—the representatives *of* slaveholders—were in the Convention that formed the Constitution of the United States, says Yancey. Moreover, says he, these men " wrote it down *in* the Constitution, that the Constitution they made, was for *themselves* and *their* posterity !"

" Were they honest and sincere? No man *dare* say to-night* that they were not! If honest and sincere, and they made that Constitution to confer the blessings of Liberty, on themselves and their posterity, then, most assuredly," exclaimed Yancey, " they never designed *that* Constitution for the *black* race, and *these* were not the men they declared to be free and equal."

There could not possibly have been framed language more insulting to the great mass of Southern white men than that used by Mr. Yancey at that time.

First, he asserts that all the members of the Convention who formed the Constitution of the United States were " slaveholders themselves."

Secondly, he asserts that they were the " representatives" of *slaveholders.*

These two assertions taken together are exactly the same as to say that there were no non-slaveholders in the Convention, either as individuals or as a represented class.

---

* At Pike's Opera, Cincinnati, October 24, 1860.

Third, he says that these slaveholders wrote it down in the Constitution, that the Constitution they formed was for *themselves and their posterity.*

This third assertion is another way of saying what he had twice said before. It also went further, and denied all participation in the "blessings of Liberty" to the *non-slaveholders*, the poor white trash who are lower than niggers.

This is again conveyed in the argument that the negro—not being present in the Convention either individually or by representation—were not the men declared to be free and equal.

If the negro was excluded from Liberty, *because* he was not in Convention, then the non-slaveholder was excluded, because he (as Mr. Yancey expressly said) was not present in that Convention.

But Mr. Yancey believes, not less than I do, that *slavery* rests upon the basis of negro-inferiority, therefore, he spoke these words against the equality of white men.

Nationally, then, Mr. Yancey considers the non-slaveholders on a level with the negro. *Politically*, the "poor white trash," like myself, for instance, were left entirely out of the Constitution of the United States, and must give way to the *privileged class*, who intended that instrument for the exclusive benefit of "*themselves and their posterity.*"

In order to show that I take no unfair advantage of Mr. Yancey, I will now proceed to notice his *actions* subsequent to his words and their con-

14*

nection with those words. As "actions speak
louder than words," the views of Mr. Yancey will
be best discovered in his actions, *coupled with his
own words*. If the domineering exclusiveness of
the cotton-planter be patent all over his speech,
his actions are the very quintessence of arrogance
and usurpation, and, as I will show, a downright
insult to every white man who does not plant cotton. Remember, too, that the "Southern Congress" indorses Mr. Yancey.

Three months and eighteen days only had elapsed after that speech, when Mr. Yancey stood up
in the State Convention at Montgomery, Alabama,
and voted for Secession. He also voted *against
leaving it to the people for a ratification*. His
opinions prevailed. He has now, having returned
from Europe, taken a seat in the Southern Congress, where he sustains his own former course.

Let us paraphrase his own language in connection with his act, substituting the Secession Convention for the Convention which framed the
United States Constitution :

"Who were the delegates to that (Secession,
Montgomery) Convention? There was *no non-
slaveholder* in that Convention which framed the
Secession ordinance. There was no hard-handed
mechanic, no hard-working non-slaveholder of
the South in that traitor crew. There was neither non-slaveholder nor mechanic in that Convention that framed the Secession ordinance. But
these men were (most emphatically) the represent-

atives of slaveholders,—slaveholders *themselves!*
—who wrote it down that the Secession ordinance
and constitution *they* made were for *themselves* and
their posterity!

"Were *they* honest and sincere? No man
(within their merciless and unauthorized control)
dare say to-night that they are not."*

If honest and sincere, and they made that ordinance and that Constitution to confer the blessings of "Southern Independence" upon *themselves*
and *their* posterity, then, most assuredly, they
never designed those documents for the non-slaveholder, and the non-slaveholder was *not* the man
they declared independent.

See upon what a shifting sand rests the fabric
of "Southern Independence" in a " Southern Confederacy!"

If a negro is unequal to a white man, *only because* he was not represented in the Convention
that framed the United States Constitution, *how
can* the non-slaveholder be equal to the slaveholder, when the former was not represented in
the *Secession* Convention *nor* in the *Southern Congress?* Mr. Yancey is a palpable advocate for
negro equality by *debasing* the *white* man, even
while he execrates those who advocate the *same
thing* by elevating the negro. *I am not a political adherent of either the one or the other ;* but, if

---

* One man did and does deny their honesty, but he writes
these words in exile.

I *must* choose between the degradation of my own race, or the elevation of the black, I prefer the latter, as the least of two evils. My conservatism, however, causes me unequivocally to condemn both forms of negro equality.

So well did Mr. Yancey reflect the true sentiments and *intentions*, against what he calls the "poor white trash," of the "slaveholding community," who employed him, that they sent him to Europe to represent "*themselves and their posterity abroad!*"

O downtrodden, deceived, betrayed, insulted "white people" of the South! those of you who have been duped into shouldering your muskets for Secession, have, through passionate blindness, helped to forge the chain which is, even now, eating away the ankles of your liberties. Poor serfs that you are, you have allowed yourselves to be "precipitated into a" political hell, from which you lack the spirit to declare *yourselves* and *your* posterity "independent."

I thank my God, that, when the impartial pen of history shall record the transactions of Alabama through the last presidential campaign and the stormy times that succeeded it, the chronicler will be compelled to admit that one, at least, of the non-slave-owners of that ill-used State, true to the principles of democracy and to his solemn and recorded oath, defended *his* equality with the planters at the peril of his life; and, in his speeches and his acts, *openly asserted* the *personal* independence of all white men to be preferable to sectional independence, *individual* equality to be better than State equality, and the *Union* which combines all the blessings Washington fought and Jefferson *thought* to secure, more to be desired than all the glittering but empty bribes of Secession! Yes! Heaven be praised, that the "former law-partner of Yancey, refusing to become his partner in crime," resisted, at the peril of his life, the unconstitutional encroachments of the aristocrats, as anti-American, and hostile to the liberties of the "people"—the "poor white trash" (as the master of the slave calls the master of no slave); and, both with pen and tongue, labored to defeat the machinations of the resident enemies of the South, and to overthrow the foul conspiracy of the advocates of "*King* Cotton!"

SCENE THE SIXTH.

_____

"IN EXILIUM."

"O unexpected stroke, worse than of death!
And must I leave thee, Paradise? *thus* leave
Thee, native soil; these happy walks and shades,
Fit haunt of gods? where I had hoped to spend.
Quiet, though sad, the respite of that day,
That must be mortal to us both."

PARADISE LOST.

"Home, kindred, friends, and country—these
Are ties with which we never part;
From clime to clime, o'er land and seas,
We bear them with us in our heart;
But oh! 'tis hard to feel resigned,
When these must all be left behind!"

J. MONTGOMERY.

IT is unnecessary to enumerate all the incidents of that night's dreary tramp. At about four o'clock, A. M., we arrived at Benton, twelve miles from the place of starting, and awaited, at "the tavern," the approach of dawn and of the steamer.

The steamer, as often occurs, *was belated.* This fact nearly cost me my life. The news spread like wildfire through the place that "a Lincoln-man*

_____

* If doing all I could to *defeat* Mr. Lincoln's election, for the sake of the Union, make me a Lincoln-man, what does my disapproval of his usurpations make me?

was in town." The population, excited by a thousand vague sensations, gathered in knots to discuss
the incredible occurrence. The news came to the
committee that the next boat would not pass before *three o'clock*, P. M. They had retired to bed,
in order to sleep, after their *patriotic* labors of the
preceding night. At this news, I demanded that
they find some other conveyance than the steam-
boat. " Why don't you swim the river, sir?"
asked one. " Because I *once* tried to swim the
river of Secession, and was washed ashore !" The
committee laughed heartily, and sent one of their
number down-stairs on a secret mission. He soon
returned, and informed them that the request was
granted. Through the windows could be seen the
gathering mob. Their wild gestures and growing
excitement were no pleasing spectacle to me.
They pointed to the house where I was a prisoner.
One of the committee was addressing them in
soothing tones. I could hear the words " severely
punished already'," and " our county has done her
share," and " other counties must," and " let him
go to Montgomery."

At the last words, a smile spread from face to
face, and significant nods and looks sent a thrill of
horror through my veins.

A hand was laid upon my shoulder :

" Mr. Tharin, would you be willing to risk the
Montgomery stage? You'll be in danger if you
stay here, and you will run a risk if you go to
Montgomery——"

"And I'll be hanged if I venture to return to Collirene!"

"Yes, sir, and your own choice must guide you."

"I'll take the stage."

"It is at the door."

Through the scowling throng which was collecting between the door and the stage, the American exile entered the vehicle, amid the growls and execrations of his rebellious fellow-citizens. The driver cracked his whip, and then, as the stage sprang forward with a bounding oscillation,—above the roar of the wheels, above the rattling of the strong harness, above the tramp of the horses, above the banging of the luggage, above the wild beating of my heart,—I heard the last shout which ever greeted my ears, in times of peace, from a Southern mob.

This, then, was the farewell which my native clime breathed to my departing form—and why?

Because I had endeavored to vindicate the inborn rights of fourteen-fifteenths of that mob, without subtracting from the equal rights of the other fifteenth.*

In other words, I had discovered an unpopular truth, for the reception of which the public mind was unprepared. The mists of error were not yet pierced by the rising sun of political enlightenment. But think not, misguided men, that by driving into exile the first Southern man who ever

---

* See p. 48, *ante.*

practically grasped the idea of the non-slaveholder's *rights* and the non-slaveholder's *power*,
that you have extinguished the holy beams of
truth, or unseated from his eternal throne that
God who dwelleth in the truth! As surely as that
God reigneth, will come a day when the clouds
will be rolled away from the door of Liberty's
temple, and the non-slaveholder shall enter there,
with the song of true Southern Rights upon his
lips. That day is *not* far distant, and perhaps
those very men who hissed his retiring form will
live to hang their heads in shame, when the returning footsteps of "the Alabama Refugee" shall
be pressed once more on his native soil, while the
secret conspirators, who "precipitated the Cotton
States into an (unnecessary) revolution," will hide
their diminished heads in the dens and caves of
public scorn !

There was no other passenger in the stage. It
was cold—at least, I had lost sleep, food, repose
of mind, and a chill, like death's breath, perme-
ated my bones. My thoughts were busy and tumultuous. While actual danger had confronted
me, I had, from necessity, concealed my fears,
and unflinchingly breasted my advancing fate;
but, now, the eyes of the mob and of the committee no longer glaring upon me, in the absence of any guard, any present peril—*reaction
came!*

To those, who have suffered days of intense
anxiety, nights of sleepless vigil, and hours of un-
15

ceasing suspense, this terrible word will require no explanation. The nerve that has met and sustained a long-continued tension, then relaxes; the will that met the crisis with unbending power, then yields to temporary prostration; the brain that energized with that sudden and wonderful inspiration imminent danger sometimes bestows, then sinks into a kind of collapse, and the heart, that seemed encased in adamant, then melts.

Through the corridors of memory rushed a host of thronging images.

I thought of my childhood's home.

In the far, far distance—beyond the tree-crowned hills on my right; beyond the turgid waters of the Alabama, now receding into the distance; beyond the brown cotton-stalks which rotted in their furrows, on both sides of the road; beyond the reach of all save imagination—was the "Queen city of the South."

On the northern extreme of the city of Charleston, S. C., stands the venerable colonial farm-house in which "the exile" drew his first breath. In and around that classic spot, had raged the conflicts of "'76," and its owner, my lineal ancestor, Col. Cunnington, had spent fortunes and poured out his blood for the freedom and equality of the very South Carolinians, some of whose unnatural sons, true to the instincts of their tory progenitors, and to the hereditary desire that "one of the royal family of England should rule over them," had wantonly sacrificed all the blessings the "whigs" of '76 had won through a seven years' war with the British and tories.

In the Claude-Loraine-glass of Memory, how plainly rose field, mill, forest, stream, and grove! Alas! would my feet never more wander through the "avenue," the "cottage lane?" Would the breezes of the "Belvidere" never more lift these storm-tossed locks with their perfumed wings? Would the jessamines still bloom where the solitudes speak in the diapason of waving pines—but never more for me? Would the mocking-birds mourn my absence? Alas! the tread of rebellion is all over that soil which, in 1776, drank the blood of my Union progenitors, and the tory descendants of tory sires will wander through the scenes of my childhood and call it the natal place of a—traitor!

God of Heaven! wither the lip that dares thus to desecrate the grave of the Revolutionary hero who died in the Union he helped to frame, the cradle of my Union father, and the monument of Francis Marion!

I—"a traitor?" To *what* am I a traitor? To the *South?* Thou liest, perjured spawn of a base tory, or degenerate offspring of a whig patriot! THE SOUTH CONSISTS OF HER SONS, and *thou* knowest, and *tremblest* when thou knowest, that the non-slaveholding population of her hills and her valleys, of her cities and her villages, far outnumber the planters, who, with brazen front, ejaculate— "*We* are the *South;*" while echo, through the lungs of Jefferson Davis, consumptively responds:

L'état,—c'est MOI!

Sorrow next washed out the flush of a just indignation; for I thought of my sacred dead! The very ashes of my father, which still repose—uneasily repose—in a Charleston sepulcher, would probably never feel the returning presence of these pilgrim feet. The funeral pall of Secession had been drawn over South Carolina, and had concealed, in a second burial, the hallowed dust of my father. That dear father had ever been a *Union* man! In 1832, when Nullification barricaded the streets of Charleston, that father acted, voted, and triumphed with the Unionists—although the only one of four brothers who was not a Nullifier. How appropriate that his son should be a Unionist in 1861, and sustain that father's and his own conscientious convictions, with the loss of every thing, save honor, men hold dear.

I felt an invisible presence with me in the stage, sustaining my spirit with sympathy and guardian love. I breathed a prayer to heaven and took fresh courage. I remembered how I had ever been a victim of the *gens patriciana* of the South, how the oligarchy had affected to despise me, or, when compelled to admit my equality, to "damn me with faint praise," and my soul grew stern with a sense of wrong.

The stage was rumbling along the lonely road,

but thought was traveling within it with a speed which human ingenuity has not yet rivaled.

Again I wandered, a buoyant youth, within the beloved precincts of my Alma Mater.

A lovely morning beams upon the Queen city of the South. Upon the porch of the College of Charleston stand a throng of students. With one exception, they are all richly dressed. The conversation is somewhat noisy. Asks one:

"Tom, when are you going to Edisto?"

"Whenever we can sell our land at Wadmalaw."

"How much do you ask?"

"Fifty thousand."

"Quite a sacrifice at that. How many negroes do you move?"

"One hundred and ten, big and little."

You should have witnessed his inflation when he gave the last answer.

"John," exclaimed a well-dressed but effeminate youth, "let's compare 'nigger rolls.'"

"Done!"

Each having given his numeral, there was but one left, who had not entered at all into the competition. To him turned the youth, who had demanded the comparison, and said, while his companions barely suppressed a titter:

"Tharin, how many niggers have *you?*"

The youth addressed was about eighteen years of age. His collegiate expenses were defrayed by his own efforts. He wrote for lawyers, and thus

15*

acquired the means to obtain his much coveted
education. He had made many sacrifices—health
among the number—for this precious boon. His
dress, although clean and neat, was unequal to
the broadcloth decorations of his bejeweled companions. Every student in the institution knew
that he was not wealthy, and his flushed cheek
and flashing eye sufficiently betokened the smart,
which had been wantonly, and not for the first or
last time inflicted upon his sensitive feelings.
Drawing himself up to his full height, he replied
in firm but low tones:

"I do not award the importance to "Ethiopian
attachments" which some do. I depend upon
what I am, not on what my father *has*. It is a
mark of a very diminutive character to triumph
over honest men because of adventitious possessions. If I can but successfully imitate the deeds
of my forefathers, I do not need to inherit their
money. I can *make* my living."

Not many years passed away, and that same
youth discovered that success in South Carolina
intrinsically depends upon those very "Ethiopian
attachments" he so heroically despised. On this
very account he had found it advisable to emi-
grate to Alabama, there to find all the pride and
arrogance of the cotton-planter, without the ex-
tenuation of the refinement of the South Carolina
patrician; and, after a stern, and, of course, un-
successful effort to maintain his own blood-bought
rights against their steady encroachments, was

now their persecuted victim, because he preferred his privileges as an American citizen to all the "glittering generalities" of Secession—clinging, like a drowning man, to the former as the only plank that could save him from the law-submerging billows of the latter.

With panoramic suddenness another scene rose before my vision:

A wife and little daughter are seated before a fire in a neighboring town. They are alone. The little girl sits by her mother's chair on a low stool, which she has placed for the purpose, her black eyes beaming with affectionate intelligence. Her mother is telling her that her father will soon return, and bring her a present, if she will be a good little girl. The child's innocent prattle fills the apartment. She is a sweet little thing about two years old, her auburn hair curling around her symmetrical head, and her little hands gesticulating gracefully, as, in musical syllables, she paints her bright thoughts.

The door opens. The child springs up and exclaims:

"Mamma, papa's come!"

But, no! it is a pale and excited face that appears at the portal—a face that brings a gloom into the room. By the magnetism of that face the child is silenced.

"Mother," cries the wife, "what's the matter?"

"Prepare yourself, my daughter, for bad news."

"Is my husband dead?" she gasps. "Tell me! oh, do not keep me in suspense!"

"He is worse than dead."

The wife falls back with an agonized shriek, the child screams and weeps with an undefined dread, and—the occupant of the stage starts up with a groan and recovers from his vision.

Suddenly the stage stops.

One of the two men on the driver's box, dismounts and comes round to the door and gazes intently at the sufferer. A tear starts involuntarily to his eye as he sees his passenger convulsively sobbing.

Returning to his place he is heard to ejaculate, "poor fellow," and the stage rolls on.

From my portmanteau I drew a pair of black pants and exchanged for them the light purple pair I then wore; drew off my overcoat and replaced my beaver hat with a light blue cloth cap.

As I was replacing the articles I had removed from the valise, my hand encountered a book, which unknown to me, some one, probably my dear mother, had placed therein. I drew it forth and gazed upon a copy of the Holy Bible. What early associations did that book recall to my mind! All the reverence of early youth was added to the interest with which I looked upon the gift. It was long before I could collect my thoughts sufficiently to view the inside. I felt a strange presentiment that the Book would say something good to my bleeding heart, and to myself I said that I would read whatever part I opened it at—hoping to open it at the Psalms of David.

I opened it carefully, and was disappointed to find before me the seventeenth chapter of the Book of the Prophet Ezekiel, which I began to read with impatience; but, as I progressed, the great significance of the chapter and its adaptation to my own views, comforted me no little. I will here insert what I that day read, and ask the reader whether it be not a remarkably correct history of this Rebellion, and a perfect description of what I shall call

THE RISE, PROGRESS, AND FALL OF KING COTTON,

Predicted, and minutely described in the Holy Bible.

EZEKIEL, CHAPTER XVII.

PARABLE OF THE TWO EAGLES.

1 And the word of the Lord came unto me, saying,

2 Son of man, put forth a riddle, and speak a parable unto the house of Israel;

[1] 3 And say, Thus saith the Lord God; A great eagle with great wings, long-winged, full of feathers, which had divers colours, came unto Lebanon, and took the highest branch of the cedar:

4 He cropped off *the top*[2] *of his young twigs*, and

---

[1] 3d v. A perfect description of the American Eagle—the national escutcheon. Congress passed resolutions on the subject. Lebanon, By metonomy, for the East. Cedar, commercial prosperity.

[2] The highest commercial prosperity.

carried it into a land of traffic[1] ; he set it in a city of merchants.

[2] 5 He took also of the seed[3] of the land, and planted it in a fruitful field ; he placed *it* by great waters, *and* set it *as* a willow-tree.

6 And it grew, and became a spreading vine of low stature, whose branches turned toward him, and the roots thereof were under him : so it became a vine, and brought forth branches, and shot forth sprigs.

[4] 7 There was also another great eagle with great wings and many feathers : and behold, this vine did bend her roots toward him, and shot forth her branches toward him, that he might water it by the furrows of her plantation.

8 It was planted in a good soil by great waters, that it might bring forth branches, and that it might bear fruit, that it might be a goodly vine.

[5] 9 Say thou, Thus saith the Lord God ; Shall it prosper ? shall he not pull up the roots thereof, and cut off the fruit thereof, that it wither? it shall wither in all the leaves of her spring, even without great power or many people to pluck it up by the roots thereof.

10 Yea, behold, *being* planted, shall it prosper ? shall it not utterly wither, when the east wind toucheth it ? it shall wither in the furrows where it grew.

---

[1] The United States.

[2] 5th, 6th, and 8th v. A perfect description of the Cotton Plant.

[3] Cotton seed, introduced into the country by congressional enactment—by the American Eagle.

[4] 7th v. The "Confederate States" under the symbol of an Eagle, seceded from the "divers colors" mentionee in v. 3, but omitted in this connection.

[5] 9th, 10th v. The downfall of Cotton predicted from Anglo-Indian competition, and, *now* let me add, the blockade.

11 ¶ Moreover the word of the Lord came unto me, saying,

12 Say now to the rebellious house,[1] Know ye not what these *things mean?* Tell *them,* Behold, *the king of Babylon*[2] is come to *Jerusalem,*[3] and hath taken the *king*[4] thereof, and the *princes*[5] thereof, and led them with him to *Babylon.*[6]

13 And hath taken of the *king's seed,*[7] and made a *covenant*[8] with him, and hath taken an *oath* of him ; *he hath also taken the mighty of the land,*

14 *That the kingdom might be base,*[9] that it might not lift itself up, *but* that by keeping of his *covenant* it might stand.

15 But he rebelled against him in sending his ambassadors into *Egypt,*[10] that they might give him horses and much people. Shall he prosper? shall he escape that doeth such *things?* or, shall he break the covenant, and be delivered?

16 *As* I live, saith the Lord God, surely in the *place*[11] *where* the *king*[12] *dwelleth* that made *him*[13] king, whose

---

[1] 11th, 12th v. Why is "the rebellious house" mentioned *here,* in connection with the two Eagles and the "spreading vine of low stature," unless the above comments be true?

[2] King Cotton.   [3] Washington.   [4] Buchanan.

[5] M. C. and cabinet.   [6] Montgomery, Alabama.

[7] John C. Breckenridge, Vice President.

[8] Secret League. Breckenridge hesitated, but finally took the oath.

[9] This word, "base," which could not otherwise be understood, is now plain.

[10] The House of Bondage, where the oppressed non-slave-owners dwell in all the beauty of negro equality.

[11] Montgomery.   [12] King Cotton.   [13] Jefferson Davis.

oath he[1] despised, and whose covenant[2] he brake, *even* with him in the midst of Babylon[3] he[4] shall die.

17 Neither shall Pharaoh[5] with *his* mighty army and great company, make for him in the war, by casting up mounts, and building forts, to cut off many persons :

18 Seeing he despised the *oath*[6] by breaking the covenant, when lo, he had given his hand, and hath done all these *things*, *he*[7] shall not escape.

19 Therefore, thus saith the Lord God ; *As* I live, surely *mine oath*[8] that he hath despised, and my covenant that he hath broken, even it will I recompense upon his own head.

20 And I will spread my net[9] upon him, and he shall be taken in my snare,[10] and I will bring him to Babylon, and will plead with him there for his trespass that he hath trespassed against me.

21 And all his fugitives with all his bands shall fall by the sword, and they that remain shall be scattered toward all winds : and ye shall know that I the Lord[11] have spoken *it*.

[12] 22 ¶ Thus saith the Lord God : I will also take of

---

[1] King Cotton.   [2] The oath of U. S. Senator.

[3] Montgomery. By 10th and 11th verses of chapter xi., changed to Richmond, Va.

[4] He (Breckenridge) shall die.   [5] Beauregard.

[6] Oath of U. S. Officer.   [7] Beauregard.

[8] The oaths of office end with " So help me God !"

[9] See 10th verse.

[10] " The wicked shall lay a snare for their own feet."

[11] 21st v. No *party*, no leader, no army, can claim the victory, but the Lord alone will create a reaction and prove to the world how insignificant are the rulers whom the American people have elevated to power.

[12] From the 22d to the 24th verses, inclusive, constitutes a

the highest branch of the high cedar, and will set *it ;* I will crop off from the top of his young twigs a tender one, and will plant *it* upon an high mountain and eminent :

23 In the mountain of the height of Israel will I plant it : and it shall bring forth boughs, and bear fruit, and be a goodly cedar : and under it shall dwell all fowl of every wing : in the shadow of the branches thereof shall they dwell.

24 And all the trees of the field shall know that I the Lord have brought down the high tree, have exalted the low tree, have dried up the green tree, and have made the dry tree to flourish : I the Lord have spoken and have done *it.*

---

promise of a better day, when "peace, unity, and concord" shall render the land again prosperous, after Radicalism shall have been abated—and in all this the emancipation of the negro is not once hinted at by the holy prophet.

The five last verses of the twentieth chapter of the same Prophet, serve as a key to the above by using the very nomenclature of these times :

"CHAP. xx., v. 45 ¶ Moreover the word of the Lord came unto me, saying,

"46 Son of man, set thy face toward the South, and drop *thy word* toward the South, and prophesy *against the forest of the South field :*

"47 And say to the *forest* of the South, Hear the word of the Lord ; Thus saith the Lord God ; Behold, *I will kindle a fire in thee,** and it shall devour every green tree in thee, and every dry tree : the flaming flame shall not be quenched, and all *faces from the South to the North shall be burned therein.*

"48 And all flesh shall see that I the Lord have kindled it : it shall not be quenched.

"49 Then said I, Ah, Lord God ! they say of me, Doth he not speak parables ?"

---

* I will fire the Southern heart.   Cotton shall be consumed.

16

At a half-way station on the road, the stage
halted for the customary change of horses. Here
I found an individual emerging from the half-way
house leading a fleet-looking horse, covered with

The Book of the Prophet Ezekiel is a received portion of
the Holy Bible. The Bible is every day held up to us as a
divine book, and yet very few persons trouble themselves as
to whether this divine book relates to them. This same care-
less and superficial view of Scripture leads many persons to
pass by the prophecies as already fulfilled or relating to the
Day of Judgment, but having no present signification whatever. The Bible, on the contrary, must refer to our country
in some part of it, or else it is a defective work. The prophet
Ezekiel has certainly given some very wonderful and correct
delineations of our own times, not only in the passages just
quoted entire, but also in the whole prophecy.

The scope of the present undertaking precludes a lengthy
commentary upon a whole division of Holy Writ ; but the
reader is merely referred to the following chapters as corrob-
orative of what has already been advanced. He will find that
they will richly repay scrutiny.

Chapters i. and x. describe, under the symbol of four cheru-
bim, the four sections of this country ; while a wheel within a
wheel, an *imperium in imperio*, describes the States contained
in the Union.

Chapters ii. and iii. The commission of Ezekiel. The roll
to be eaten was the Constitution of the United States.

Chapters iv., v., vi., vii. A miserable picture of disunion
and its bloody effects.

Chapter viii. Jealousy of the North, and mobocracy in the
South. Verse 16, foreign intervention asked. Removal of
capital from Montgomery to Richmond, Va. The punishment
of Rebellion described.

Chapter xiii. The Secession orators rebuked.

Chapter xiv. The negro idolaters of the North rebuked.
The Nativity of the United States, and her prostitution to the

foam. He rested his eyes upon me, and seemed to approve of my general appearance, for he smiled and nodded kindly as he said :

" Mister, where do you intend to go to !"

" I'm bound for Montgomery."

" Where are you from ?"

" I am from Charleston, whither I will soon return."

" I have a fine horse here, you may have cheap. *Maybe you will need him before you get very far from here.*"

" I am not prepared to purchase now. I don't think I will need a horse very soon; but he is a noble animal.

" He is only six years old, and of good breed. You may have him for ninety dollars; I have a *strong* saddle and bridle you can buy for fifteen."

"almighty dollar." Verse 46, Samaria, intended to mean Mexico.

Chapter xviii. Repentance will be met with mercy.

Chapters xxvi., xxvii., xxviii. England's power and ruin graphically described.

Chapters xv., xxii. Minute description of the rise, progress, and fall of King Cotton.

Chapters xxxi., xxxii. Minute description of the power of King Cotton, and the lamentations of his admirers over his fall.

Chapter xxxiii. An exhortation to the people of the whole country.

Chapter xxxiv. The pulpit politicians rebuked, North and South.

Chapter xxxv. France and her rapacious policy denounced.

Chapters xxxvi., xxxvii., xxxix. Reunion beautifully described.

"A bargain, no doubt; but I am not purchasing this evening."

"*Any time in two days*, you can find him in Montgomery, if you want him. Enquire for John Raymond, and you'll find me."

"Very well, I will remember that."

"You say you're from Charleston? How are they getting on at Fort Sumter?"

Looking with scrutiny upon my interlocutor, I said:

"We're 'casting up mounts and building forts to cut off' Anderson's supplies. The lighted match is already held over the touch-hole. The first gun of a mighty revolution may even now be booming across the Bay. How are you affected at the prospect out here?"

A curious smile flitted across his face, as the stranger said in a voice which was as much like a taunt as a certain covert exultation could render it:

"Bully for you!"

I felt the startled blood rush from my face to my heart, which beat a rat-tat-too against my side —*was I discovered?*

My feelings were not rendered pleasanter by the suppressed laughter of the two stage-drivers, who evidently heard every word.

I was reassured, however, by the discovery that my interlocutor seemed as much annoyed by the eavesdropping as myself.

"Have you much experience in horses?" I demanded, in order to escape the oppressive silence.

"I used to drive the stage on the Nashville and Chattanooga line."

Soon the 'stage was on its way Montgomery-ward. I looked back from the window, and saw John Raymond saddling his horse, and gazing at the stage with an excited air, to me inexplicable. His motions were convulsive and hurried, and he seemed fevered by some secret emotion which, at times, broke out into kicks administered to his spirited steed.

Could it be, thought I, that all this indignation was the result of my refusal to purchase his horse?

I drew no good augury from this mental reply:

"He must be a spy!"*

After about a half-hour's ride, one of the men in front called aloud to me to come outside, as I would suffer, if I did not, from the rough "puncheon" or "corduroy" road we were about to traverse. Not desiring to be visible to passers-by, I declined. The invitation was repeated at various points on the road, until, finding my re-fusal annoyed the men, I went out and ran the gauntlet of about a mile, when, complaining of the cold, I re-entered the stage.

A significant look passed between my conduc-tors as I sprang into the coach, which was not particularly gratifying to my feelings. I began to doubt their disposition to serve a fellow-creature

---

* How often have I had the same suspicion when convers-ing with Northern Radicals!

in distress; but I resolved to show no mortification or displeasure at their manners toward myself.

Of course, invention was busy in my brain as to what I should do upon my arrival at the capital of the so-called Confederate States. I was well known at Montgomery among the public men; but these were the very men to avoid, not to apply to.

To illustrate the danger I was about to encounter, I must here digress from the thread of my narrative to a scene not very long antecedent to the point the reader has reached.

The Democratic State Convention had sent its delegates to what many of them fondly hoped would prove the *last* of the National Conventions of that party,* and, in consequence of the predetermined disruption of the Charleston Convention, another Democratic Convention had been assembled at Montgomery, " to see what was best to be done."

To that large Convention I was a delegate and offered a series of resolutions to the Assembly, advocating a proposition by Alabama to her sister States, North and South, for a National Convention, for the purpose of proposing *amendments* to the Constitution of the United States.

During the speech which, in favor of peaceful and conciliatory measures, I attempted to make,

---

* But, by the grace of God, that hope will doubtless be frustrated.

there was a universal confusion. The Convention was not permitted to listen because certain emissaries of Yancey passed rapidly around the room, and informed the audience in audible stage-asides that *Yancey wanted to speak.* I had not spoken more than three minutes, when the whole Convention became convulsed with stormy excitement. Cries of " Yancey," " Yancey !" shook the dome of the capitol. Finding it in vain to· proceed in the teeth of so strong a determination to reject my resolutions without a hearing, I exclaimed :

" *One* word, if you please—*only one !* Words of wisdom *sometimes* fall from the lips of persons who are unblessed with plantations. If cotton *must* be *King* here, and, if none but his *courtiers* can speak (cries of " none else," and " Yancey"), let the *result* be noted on the page of history. I wash my hands of all personal responsibility. *Proceed with your wild work.* Youthful prudence retires abashed from the presence of hoary " precipitancy."

Mr. Yancey, amid an ovation of applause, then rose, and advocated his own views, to the delight of the courtiers of his " King." He was not as happy in his speech as usual ; but he had won the approbation of the cotton-planters by his anti-democratical course in Charleston, and was applauded to the echo by those whose unconstitutional power he was so ably supporting.

Having temporarily ceased to act with the

Democratic Party, which, during the period of its dislocation, could not effect any thing for the Union which I had sworn to support,—but to which party I now publicly and solemnly renew my adherence, as to the only one which possesses within itself the ingredients of Nationality and Union,—I spoke during the subsequent canvass in Montgomery before the Bell-Everett club, and advocated the Union as the only salvation of Alabama and of the South. The Montgomery *Advertiser*—Yancey's organ—had then made me the object of spiteful vituperation, and, afterward, the frequent contributions, over my own name, in the Montgomery *Post* (Bell-Everett), and the *Confederation* (Douglas), had not made me less known than I was otherwise rendered by my former law-partnership with Yancey himself.

I said invention was busy in my brain as to my course after I should have found myself in the Confederate capital. In vain I strove to think of a single chance of escape. To go home was out of the question. Although but fourteen miles, by land, from Montgomery, Wetumpka was the most dangerous place to me in Alabama. I do not think any of its inhabitants would have harmed me—unless some fanatical planter like Dr. Penick,—who, *of course*, would seek my destruction, seeing he had never forgiven me for my exposure of his mobocrasy,—or some tool of King Cotton, such as Bob Clark,—who, after inciting the youth of Wetumpka to enlist against their government, refused to expose his forfeit life in their company,—could have been so base as to perpetrate the murderous deed. But the roads to my residence were sure to be blockaded by the secret emissaries of Robert Rives and his coadjutors, who were evidently determined to assassinate me.

It was clear I must not remain in Alabama, because, nowhere could I find adequate protection —not even among my Union confreres of Coosa county, who were unarmed and unprepared for self-defence. I determined not to involve my friends in a bootless danger. I *must* temporarily leave Alabama!

But how? My decision must be *quickly* formed. My mind, it is true, did revert to scenes where a friendship was formed which can never die. For not asking aid of that friend, whose name, although engraved upon the tablets of my heart, must not be written here, my apology must be that I would have perished a thousand times before I would have involved my friend in danger.

And yet, thought recoiled upon itself, whenever it essayed to discover any other means of escape. In that modern Babylon, there was no refuge from King Cotton, except in acknowledging his omnipotent sway. This I had not done— would never do. I was even then fleeing from his vengeance. His dreadful form, like a modern Colossus of Rhodes, seemed to bestride the city, whose steeples and capitol loomed up in the distance against the starlit sky. His awful decrees

were, even then, pronounced from the Exchange,
and fell, in thunder, upon the ears of sovereign
States, who respectfully removed their glittering
coronets and laid them at his feet. The gas-lights
of the city, becoming visible, seemed the Argus-
eyed guardians of his power. As we drew nearer,
the occasional stroke of a Sabbath bell melodiously
summoned the inhabitants to their evening praises.
The venial clergy would soon be busy in exhort-
ing his subjects to obey the behests of a king, upon
whose head is denounced the vengeance of the
Most High God, in Ezekiel, xvii. 19.

There lay the great Babylon of the Western
World, like a beast of prey crouching for a spring
at the throat of every Alabamian who still loved
the national Union, respected his oath, and reject-
ed the claims of the usurper " King Cotton."

I could not but feel the awful proximity of that
city weighing upon my life.

While filled with the most gloomy reflections,
I was roused from my meditations by the clatter-
ing hoofs of an approaching horse. Nearer and
nearer came the rider, until close to the vehicle,
where he reined up for a moment, scrutinized the
stage and especially its inside occupant, when,
seeming satisfied with the survey, he again put
spurs to his horse, raised a derisive whoop, waved
aloft his cap, and darted into the city at the top
of his speed.

I recognized John Raymond on his foaming
steed.

My position was critical in the extreme. This man was about to rouse the town for my warm reception. As we rumbled into the "city of the great king," my heart fainted within me. My worst enemy could not wish me to be in a more utterly abject state of hopelessness. My friends, alas! knew not even where I was at that moment. The news of my victimization could not possibly have reached my *friends* even in Montgomery, much less Wetumpka. The good, who dwelt in the capital of King Cotton, could not—the wicked would not—interpose the outraged law for my protection.

The stage suddenly stopped. We had entered the city through a suburb unseen by me before. One of the men dismounted from the driver's box, and coming to the door, said:

"Mister, I'm going to stop here, and perhaps you'd like to get out too. This is a private house, and here you can be accommodated about as well as anywhere else. If you don't like the place after you get here, you can change it, you know, and I'll help you make a selection."

There was genuine kindness in the tones. I consented. As we entered the house, I turned toward the street, and received a bow from the ubiquitous John Raymond, who rode composedly by, singing these words, which I did not *then* understand:

" When the devil was sick, the devil a saint would be,
When the devil was well, the devil a *saint* was he."

A derisive laugh formed the chorus.

Was it the chilliness of the evening, or this new cause for watchfulness which sent a cold shudder through my frame, as I drew near the blazing oak fire?

The lady of the house, about forty years of age, was blessed with the society of four or five handsome daughters. Between the stage-driver and his wife—at least his affectionate manner seemed to point out his interlocutrix as such—was conducted a whispered conversation, the result of which was a warm supper for the guest.

My respectful manner brought an astonished expression to their faces. One of the young ladies sat beside me, held my plate, smiled upon me, and asked me whether "any thing ailed" me; "for," said she, "you are thoughtful and silent." Raising my eyes, they encountered a pair of beautiful brown orbs resting upon them with an expression which caused me involuntarily to smile in return; but it was a sad, sad smile; so much so that my fair companion exclaimed:

"Something *does* ail you! You look miserable." Then, lowering her voice, she whispered: "Confide in me."

There was a sudden inclination in my thought to tell her all; to claim her sympathy as a woman, and obtain her aid for my escape; but, swallowing the sob which human sympathy was evoking, I forced myself to say:

"Although I am much obliged to you for your

sympathy, I can not tell you my troubles. They involve important secrets."

" Well, well, your secret shall not be invaded. But cheer up, man! Don't look so heartbroken."

This was said with an odd admixture of playfulness, petulance, and pity, and soon the refugee and his pretty tormentor were conversing more freely together.

But time was precious. Reminding William, as the ladies called the driver, that I must be going, I was about to leave, when the former caught Hatty to his heart, gave her a pronounced kiss, then started off with his quondam passenger.

" You do not seem to have been long married, sir," I innocently remarked.

A loud laugh shook William's frame, as, slapping me familiarly upon the back, he exclaimed—

" Come along, man ; you're green!"

I could not forbear to mingle a smile with the conscious flush which attended my conviction that I had unconsciously entered one of those gilded portals which introduce so many of our race to the vestibule of ruin.

" *Honi soit qui mal y pense.*"

17

SCENE THE SEVENTH.

" THE CITY OF THE GREAT KING."*

" For now I stand as one upon a rock,
    Environed by a wilderness of sea,
    Who marks the waxing tide grow, wave by wave,
    Expecting ever when some envious surge
    Will, in his brinish bowels, swallow him."

ON the plea of business at the Exchange hotel,
the fugitive left his companion at a crossing, and
found himself—alone!

Think of it! a Unionist of 1861, outlawed, hunted, wearied, despairing, in the streets of the Confederate capital—*alone!*

Say! can you imagine a situation of more total
abandonment? Is there, on God's green footstool,
a spot more dangerous to human tread, than the
streets of Montgomery *then*† were to the presence
of R. S. Tharin?

The crater of Vesuvius is not inaccessible to
human visitation, when the soft breezes whisper
through its caverns, and the vine-bearing hills lift
their summits in the purple sunset; but, when the
lava-waves of Nature's fiercest convulsion wrap

---

* Cotton.   † Not so to be always, however.

city and forest in lurid glare, while the rocking
earth hurls fragmentary temples from their bases
—*then?*

Why, then! to tread upon the brink of that
earthly hell, is quite a different thing!

It is the holy Sabbath eve (February 24th, 1861),
and Montgomery's Christian temples are pouring
out their retiring congregations under the peaceful
stars. Reverend gentlemen, with snowy cravats
and mincing gait, walk in the midst of gayly
dressed damsels, who court their clerical smiles;
elders and vestrymen, Sunday-school teachers and
exhorters, laymen and deacons, presbyters and
bishops—how multitudinously their feet patter, or
strut, or stamp, or scrape, over that gas-lit pave!
To see the happy throng, you would suppose them
all to be on a starlit promenade *direct* to heaven,
and that this pave is the "narrow way."

But you would be mistaken; for this—although
quiescent—is Vesuvius still!

Should that mincing Pharisee, the cut of whose
orthodox garment proclaims the clerical Brum-
mell, as he saunters by with virgin innocence
resting upon his arm, detect the presence, and its
cause, of that traveler who, portmanteau in hand,
is crossing toward the line of the Christian cara-
van, his lips, yet warm with pulpit strains of peace,
and rhetorical flourishes about the *mob* of Calvary, would sound the tocsin of persecution; and
his delicate hands, yet red with pummeling the
gospel according to St. Matthew, or the martyr-

dom of St. Stephen, would hold the garments of
those who would arrange the martyr's noose
around a patriot's neck, consenting to—his death!

Should that delicate female, whose intellectual
brow is crowned with golden ringlets, and whose
celestial eyes are upturned with worship to meet
the rapt glance of her spiritual guide—should she
perceive that a friend of the Union of her forefathers had just passed by, with mingled rage and
hate she would shriek aloud, and the cry—*false
as hell!*—"Abolitionist! hang him!" would be
the chivalrous response. "At that cry accurst,"
the heavenward throng would pause, attent, upon
the "narrow way," and, catching up the celestial
sound, would spring upon the fugitive's path like
bloodhounds after their prey. Should their chase
be crowned with success, they would add another
element of thanksgiving to their next Sunday's
praises, and lift their blood-stained hands to
heaven, in attestation of their pious devotion to
that Cotton who (for them) is supreme "in heaven
above, in earth beneath, and in the waters that
are under the earth."

Alone, then, and—*because* loyal and law-abiding
—outlawed and hunted—an American citizen, in
his own country, stood upon the crater of a muttering volcano. Humble though he was—unblessed with wealth—is there not something anom-
alous in the situation? Can you not almost see
the forms of the great tutelaries of America, who
lived, bled, and died *in* and *for* the Union, bend-

ing from on high to keep watch over his destinies?
And *he*, the father of that exile, was not excluded
from that august band, as he watched over the
steps of his persecuted son, while the enemies of
American equality were lurking in wait for his
life.

Time was precious. I felt the precarious nature
of my footing. The only visible sympathizers
with my agony were the—stars! whose distant,
but encouraging eyes seemed to say, "Look up!"
I tried to look up, and beheld the accursed flag of
Secession, to me henceforth the detestable emblem
of *stripes* alone, flaunting from the very building
I was about to enter; but I was glad to see the
twinkling *stars* beyond and *above* it, shining se-
renely in the "azure dome of night," out of the
reach of treason or of change. They seemed to
invite—to beckon me, saying—

"Come up hither, where the stars are free!"

Have I not obeyed their mute but eloquent
invitation? Am I not enjoying a hard-earned
semi-tranquillity in the light of that constellation
which still sheds its loyal rays upon the national
banner? When the stars of heaven fell, the powers that were in heaven were only "shaken."
Passed is now the convulsion, and the pillars of
Liberty rock only on account of a recent vibration.

"It was (*mirabile dictu!*) into the Exchange
hotel that I was about to enter. In that hotel,
the perjured members of the illegitimate "Southern Congress" were even then concocting their

17*

flagitious schemes for the overthrow of that government the loyal citizen was risking his very life to maintain.

The editor of the Charleston *Mercury* and one of the members of the "Southern Congress" are the sole occupants of "No. 6."

A muffled knock is heard at the door, and in response to the invitation "come in," a pallid face and eager eyes burst upon the twain.

The member of the Southern Congress rises and extends his hand:

"Mr. Tharin, how *do* you do? Where have you come from? You look badly, but I can never forget that face."

"Mr. Miles, I have come far to see you, and would prefer to communicate with you *alone*."

Exit R. Barnwell Rhett, Jr., editor of the Charleston *Mercury*.

As this man has played a conspicuous part in hounding on *his class*,—the cotton aristocrats,—advocating every species of excess in the polished periods of a cultivated pen, it may not be amiss to give a short sketch of his *origin*, of which he is very proud.

In 1712–13 the Tuscaroras, Corees, and other Indian tribes in North Carolina, broke out into sudden hostilities against the white settlers along the Neuce and Roanoke rivers. The "Palatines" of the old North State, then under colonial vassalage to Great Britain, could not sustain themselves without assistance, and a swift messenger was dis-

patched to Port Royal (South Carolina) for aid.
The "Lords Proprietors" sent Col. Barnwell, with
a large force (eight or nine hundred, I think),
to reduce the Indians to submission. He found
them intrenched in a fort of palisades. Being
afraid to attack them, Barnwell entered into a
treaty with them.

On his return march he invaded certain peaceable Indian villages, and, *contrary to the stipulations of the treaty*, kidnapped not a few of the
inhabitants, whom he *imported* into South Carolina, *as slaves*, to till the indigo-fields of that
colony.*

R. Barnwell *Smith*, not more than a dozen or
two years ago, *changed his name* to Rhett, *for an
inheritance*. R. Barnwell Rhett, Jr.,—*né* Smith,
—is the hopeful scion of this most illustrious house.

But all is not yet told. In consequence of the
outrage against civilization committed by Col.
Barnwell, the massacres of the Neuce river were
renewed, when the Lords Proprietors of South
Carolina sent a smaller body of men, most of them
Indians (in the whole six hundred there were not
more than fifty whites), under Col. James Moore,
afterward governor of the colony, who *stormed* the
same fort, under more difficult circumstances, and
reduced the Indians to complete quiescence.

He committed no outrages on the return march,
and so the peace was lasting.

---

* See Carroll's Historical Collections of South Carolina.

Barnwell, the coward, faltered in attacking the
fort; Barnwell, the pirate, kidnapped peaceful
Indians as slaves for his indigo-fields.

From this distinguished slave-pirate is descended
the modern advocate of the world-wide execrated
" African slave-trade."

There is a wonderful persistency in blood to
betray its origin! This is exemplified in the life
and writings of R. Barnwell Rhett, Jr.

From this short digression, begging the reader's
pardon, return we to No. 6 Exchange Hotel,
Montgomery, after its evacuation by the editor of
the Charleston *Mercury*, the " organ" of the "first
families" of South Carolina.

The following conversation then took place :

THARIN. " Honorable William Porcher Miles,
once of the Federal, *now* of the Confederate Congress, have you forgotten 'auld lang syne?'   Do
you remember when my class at college, the College of Charleston—*your alma mater and my alma
mater*—presented the assistant professor of Mathe-
matics with a silver cup ?"

MILES. " I have not the bad taste to forget
it."

THARIN. "It was a handsome gift! It ought to
be a link between the past and the present."

MILES. " It is! it is!"

THARIN. " I'm sure, professor, if *you* were in
danger, not one of that class would refuse to save
you if he could !"

MILES. " Ah! I see! I see! *You* are in danger!

I perceive it in your whole manner. Dear pupil confide in me. What can I do for you?"

Tharin. "Save me!"

Miles. "How? when? where? why?"

Tharin. "By aiding me on my way to Cincinnati, immediately!"

Miles. "But why?"

Tharin. "An infuriated mob has already visited me with undeserved barbarities. Other mobs are gathering for my destruction. I am a fugitive from mobocracy! Will you save me?"

Miles. "What have you done?"

Tharin. "Nothing wrong."

Miles. "What is the nature of your offense?"

Thaein. "Political!"

Miles (with a darkening brow). "Ha!"

Tharin. "I was about publishing, in this city, a newspaper to be called the ' *Non-slaveholder.*'"

Miles (starting to his feet). "Good Heaven!"

Tharin. "My only object, professor, was to advocate the rights of that class to representation and equality."

Miles. "Worse and worse!—I can't help you, Mr. Tharin,—wait here a minute or two."

The victim of mobocracy had learned, by bitter experience, to read the dark thoughts of men by the light of their own eyes. There was a glitter in the glance of Miles which revealed, like the lightning from a black sky, the abyss below. Without awaiting his return, I made my way into

the street, and was about to proceed, with rapid
steps along the pavement, when, suddenly stepping
from the side of the door, a man lightly laid his
detaining fingers upon my arm.

"Stop, Mister!"

With a sudden movement, I was about to grasp
my captor's throat. My instantaneous discovery
of John Raymond did not diminish my energy,
when, in a conciliating tone, he said:

"Step this way, Mr Tharin."

"Who told you that was *my* name?"

He drew me gently to the shade of a lamp.
Then, glancing cautiously around, he said in an
almost whisper:

"I was at Collirene both times you were mobbed. I *was* not a member of the vigilance committee, or of your association, but I *am* now, by
G—! I made up my mind to follow and to save
you!" Here his voice grew thick and his breathing hard. "I got to Benton in time to prevail on
the stage-driver to take you on. I took a short
cut across the country and met you at the half-
way-house. You know the rest. To be seen in
your company now would be certain death. *You*
will be hung as high as Haman if you stay in the
State. Don't think, for a moment, of going to
your own town (Wetumpka), for you are to be
waylaid. Don't stay here another moment. You
know very well that this hole is full of your enemies. Go to Montgomery Hall, register your
name, call for a room, and, to-morrow I'll call for

you in a hack and take you to the depot of the West Point railroad."

" Many—many thanks for your—"

" Hold your—hush. You're foolish ! People's passing !"

We separated.

When I reached the hotel he had indicated, I advanced, with a beating heart, to the register, upon which I entered this fictitious name :

" B. T. Haman, Charleston, S. C.," and called for a room.

And now, if any Secessionist ventures to deny my statement, thus I prove its correctness, and the danger to which I was subjected, on account of my loyalty :

Take the hotel register of the Montgomery Hall for Sunday the 24th of February, look at the end of the arrivals for that day, and you will find the name " B. (better) T. (take), Haman, Charleston, S. C." You won't find the words " better take," but you *will* will find their initials, " B." and " T."

Again : in order to place the matter beyond the possibility of a doubt, I will here describe the very way, the surname is written

H–a–y–m–a–n.

The " y" was added, in order to prevent any association of ideas from pointing me out until too late to destroy me *and my testimony* forever.

" Now,"—thought I, as I entered that room, from which I might never emerge alive,—" now, if John Raymond meant to catch me by advising me to register my *own* name, I have completely foiled him—that's all! If he be a friend indeed, to-morrow he shall find me."

I drew off my boots, disencumbered myself of my coat and seizing the candle approached the mirror, with a vague notion that I must have changed some little in the last two or three days.

I started at the spectral face which presented itself before me. Want of rest, food, and mental peace, nights of intense misery, doubt, anxiety, suspense, hope, fear, unceasing thought, had done their work. Replacing the candle, I threw myself upon my bed, but how could I sleep? Burying my face in the pillow, I thus meditated:

"Had I commenced with perjury and ended with murder; had I been guilty of some flagrant act of violence upon the constitutional rights of some unprotected poor white man; had I accompanied the act with language of brutal contempt; had I precipitated the low and fiendish rabble to persecute, upon suspicion, a helpless wretch 'for the sake of the example'—I had, this night, been rewarded with office, popularity, and applause. But I have dared to do an act more just than popular, to keep my heaven-registered *oath*, to support the Union, the Constitution, and the cause of the defenseless and oppressed, and ―― *here* am I! a violent death closing upon me from a circumference of horror. In the center of that circle, almost overpowered with the mightiness of the crisis—too soon to give way beneath a load of woe and distress, growing, every moment, more and more intolerable, I must not make a single false step. My wife and daughter, only fourteen miles off, I may never more behold! Little do they think to-night how much I suffer. May God protect my Mollie; may he watch my little Claudia's unfolding heart and mind. O God! save us all to meet in other lands, where barbarism has given place to an enlightened civilization!"

Just then, through the corridor, I heard the approach of trampling feet.

"Suppose," said Apprehension, "suppose John Raymond should prove false. Suppose he should bring with him a brutal mob, and betray the fugitive with a kiss."

The feet came to the very door—they stopped—there came a loud rap, which was echoed in the caverns of my bosom.

"Is Mr. Haman in?"

With the inward ejaculation, "If I die for my principles, it shall not be by the felon's rope!" I opened wide the door and approached the open window as the party entered.

First appeared a negro waiter, candle in hand; then a well-dressed, but not prepossessing, gentleman; and then slowly, but excitedly, John Raymond himself.

"That will do, boy," said Raymond, and the negro retired.

With one bound he put down the window, with his back to which he stood confronting me.

"Tharin, put on your coat and boots; here, take your luggage, let me have your money, and —follow me."

I watched the quivering muscles of his face, and said:

"Do you come as a friend, or as an enemy?"

"As a friend. Follow me!"

"Your hand, in token of honest friendship, and I'll go."

Raymond saw my emotion and nervously whispered:

"Quick, quick man, we're loosing precious moments—follow me!"

"How do I know your intentions?"

Here Raymond could stand it no longer. He not only clasped my hand but my form; he wept, as a strong manly heart alone could weep.

"D—n you! come, be quick! My heartstrings are breaking for you! I *will* save you! D—n me if I don't. But I'm afraid you'll be recognized down-stairs. Your excited appearance has created a great deal of gossip down there already. Give me your money! I'll pay the bill, while you, with Mark here, slip out."

Was it a dream? Was I awake? Would I be permitted to again behold God's beautiful world? to see in it those I loved? It was too much. For one brief moment, consciousness almost forsook me in my delirious joy!

Almost without knowing how, I again found myself in the gas-lit streets of the Confederate capital, with my two companions, one on each side of me. We soon arrived at a place which I will not here describe, on account of the persecutions to which my friends might be subjected. Up stairs we groped, through the darkness, to a comfortable room, where we found ourselves soon in one bed. There were other beds in the room, but we wished to converse.

The first word I had ever heard Raymond's singular companion say was, after we were under the coverlid,

"Fools!"

"Who?" asked Raymond.

"You, and this other man. Why the devil couldn't you leave Montgomery Hall without hugging and crying like women?"

"Never mind, Mark; you go to sleep, now."

"Well, don't *cry* any more, John."

"You be d—d!" said the latter.

That was their "good-night!"

George was soon snoring in the most unequivocal manner.

I was myself rapidly sinking into the deep sleep of exhaustion, when a hand shook my shoulder, and Raymond's voice whispered,

"Are you asleep?"

"Almost."

"Wake up!"

"What's the matter?"

"When George and I leave you in the morning, he will go to his work—I'll come back with a

hack; step boldly into it and ride to the depot,
buy a ticket—it will be *early*. Take your place in
the car, and then—take care of yourself!"

"I will do as you tell me."

"And now go to sleep. Feel no dread—you're
safe. You *need* sleep—take it while you can!"

These refreshing words added fragrance to my
slumber. My visions were the thoughts of Innocence, as my actions had been her suggestions.
No Abolition incendiarism filled my dreams with
the charred remains of conflagrated houses; but
the white dove of returning peace nestled over the
land, the curtain of futurity lifted, and Alabama
emerged upon the stage of action, crowned with
the star-spangled glories of her first love, and
purified from her sin!

The next morning, two persons stood together
in a chamber in the "City of the Great King." A
hack was at the door, its negro driver composedly
seated in front, its door open, and clouds of vapor
rising from the expanding nostrils of its bay horses.
The hands of the two men were warmly inter-
clasped. He who held a portmanteau was saying—

"And we may never, on earth, meet again; but
as you have done to me, in this awful crisis of my
life, may God do to you, in your greatest need,
and more too. Never—never will I forget you!
Good-by!"

The sincere warmth with which this was said
brought a quiver to the other's lip. With clo-

quent eyes, but silent lips, he pressed the Refugee's hand, then vanished out of the door. As he went noisily, but rapidly, down the steps, his voice was overheard exclaiming—

"D—n it all! I'm getting fond of the fellow!"

Noble! kind-hearted! *patriotic* man! when God shall number his jewels, many a wealthy and refined cotton-planter, who, by virtue of a fortunate marriage or a lucky descent, now lords it over God's green heritage, shall be weighed in the balances and found wanting; while *thou*, the poor neglected stage-driver, whose earthly opportunities never equaled theirs, will hear these gracious words from a King more to be dreaded than King Cotton:

"Come, thou blessed of my Father, inherit the kingdom prepared for thee from the foundation of the world; for I was an hungered, and thou gavedst me meat; I was thirsty, and thou gavedst me drink; I was naked, and thou clothedst me; I was sick, and *in prison*, and thou didst minister unto ME."

Then, covered with modest confusion, thou shalt say:

"Lord, *when* saw I *thee* an-hungered, or a-thirst, or naked, or sick, or in prison, and ministered unto thee?"

Then shall the King of kings reply:

"Inasmuch as thou didst it to this, the least of these my brethren, thou didst it unto ME."

18*

Where, *then*, shall the conspirator, William Porcher* Miles, appear?

Methinks I hear the thunder-tones of the last Judge pronouncing these words:

"Depart from me, accursed, into everlasting fire, prepared for the devil and his angels" (*i. e.*, for the first Seceder and his followers); "for I was hungry, and thou gavedst me no meat; I was thirsty, and thou gavedst me no drink; I was sick and in prison, and thou visitedst me not. Inasmuch as thou didst it not to this, the least of these, my brethren, thou didst it not to ME!"

Then, while the humble stage-driver shall be carried to the skies in a triumphal procession of the holy angels, the crest-fallen ex-congressman, arm in arm with Jefferson Davis and William L. Yancey, will *secede* into that outer darkness congenial to their political antecedents.

Reader, do you want a friend?

Go not to the proud Pharisee, who stands at the corners of the streets that men may *see* him pray; but betake yourself to the stall and the shamble, where honest poverty wrestles with fate, and from her reluctant palm extorts a scanty subsistence. Go not to the happy and the *refined;* the cry of anguish shocks their delicate ears, and their hearts prefer to break over the imaginary sufferings of "Uncle Tom," rather than to "minister to minds diseased, pluck from the soul a rooted sorrow, and

---

* Pronounced *Porsháy.*

rid the spirit of that perilous stuff that weighs upon the heart." Above all, go not to a perjured, partisan demagogue; for, if a man be untrue to his country and his oath, how can he be true to the dictates of humanity?

We may never meet again on earth, but the daguerreotype of John Raymond shall ever remain bright in the picture-gallery of memory.

Having run the gauntlet of Main-street in the hack, I approached the depot. A gilded sign, reddening in the rays of morning, met my view. In mocking syllables, its ample letters arranged themselves before my eyes:

CHILTON & YANCEY.

Yancey! the ablest and the most unscrupulous man that ever plotted the overthrow of popular rights! The cotton aristocracy could not, by any possibility, have *produced such* a man. Originally created in God's own image, with qualities the most engaging, powers the most wonderful, genius the most transcendant, he seemed one of those whom nature throws off in her most inspired moods, and crowns with every talent that can add dignity to the forum or enthusiasm to the populace. But she had not adjusted her gifts with that nice equipoise which is essential to harmony and perfection. His ambition she made greater than his love of truth, and just a fraction larger than his vanity. Mr. Yancey commenced his political career at Cahawba, and afterward removed

to Wetumpka, where he became the editor of the
Wetumpka *Argus*. Working his way to Congress by means of that paper, he placed himself
among the "yeas and nays" in favor of the annex-
ing of the "Wilmot Proviso" to the admission of
Oregon. Reflecting afterward the political sentiments of the men upon whom he depended for
promotion, nothing became too self-contradictory
for him to do, if it but served his ultimate end.
I have heard him say (at the Commercial Convention at Montgomery, Alabama, in 1858) that he
resigned his place in Congress, in consequence of
his inability to support his family at Washington.
This proves that the cotton aristocracy did not
produce him, as I have already intimated.

His inventive genius being ever on the alert
for his own aggrandizement, the coronation of
Cotton soon placed him in the category of the
"King's" most humble subjects. Uncottoned himself, he paid his court to the wealthy courtiers of
the woolly monarch, and, by his unscrupulous ad-
hesion to His Majesty, won the post of Grand Champion of his throne. Inflated by the popularity
which he received from the dispensers of public
favor,—the planters,—there was no deed too black,
no means too corrupt for the achievement of his
ends.* What would have been in a good cause,

---

* "MONTGOMERY, June 15, 1858.
"DEAR SIR:—

"Your kind letter of the 15th is received. I hardly agree
with you that a general movement can be made that will clean

sustained by truth, a divine enthusiam, was in the mind of a perjurer, but the excitement of ambition in its hot pursuit of personal success.

It is my firm conviction that Mr. Yancey s ambition aspires to *the throne itself*. What easier for an eloquent man, after filling the public tongue with the enthusiastic monosyllable "King," applied to an invisible but omnipresent idea, than to

---

out the Augean Stable. If the *Democracy* were overthrown, it would result in giving place to a greater and *a hungrier swarm of flies*.

"The remedy of the South is not in such a process. It is in a diligent organization of her true men for the prompt resistance of the next aggression. It must come in the nature of things. No national party can save us, no sectional party can ever do it. But, if we should do as our fathers did—*organize committees of safety all over the Cotton States* (and it is only in *them* we can hope for any effective movement),—we shall fire the Southern heart, instruct the Southern mind, give courage to each other, and, at the proper moment, by one organized, concerted action, we can *precipitate* the Cotton States into a revolution.

"The idea has been shadowed forth in the South by Mr. Ruffin,—has been taken up and recommended by the *Advertiser* under the name of 'League of United Southerners,' who, keeping up the old party relations on all other questions, will hold the Southern issue paramount, and will influence parties, Legislatures, and statesmen. I have no time to enlarge, but to suggest merely.

"In haste,   Yours, &c.,

"W. L. YANCEY.

"To JAMES SLAUGHTER, Esq."

Dr. Slaughter, having published the above "*private letter*," as Mr. Yancey afterward called it, was found dead in his bed from the effects of *poison!*

fill that same tongue with his own name, as the main prop of the monarchy, and, in the absence of any tangible superstructure, to become the very "King" in name he had already become in substance. There is no question in my mind that Jefferson Davis also beholds the same glittering vision. Alexander H. Stephens, had retired to private life, until the mandate of " *King* Cotton" called him forth to contradict himself, for a promotion higher than any he had ever before dreamed of.

The abilities of William L. Yancey will ultimately make him the first in the Confederacy, unless a reaction occurs, which could easily be produced by the rise of a National party in the North. From the non-slaveholders he has stolen their rights; but he has made the slaveholders his dupes, his instruments — for they are his only beneficiaries. He is ever wedded to *their* interests, and they to *his* by the base disintegration of the Democratic party, at Charleston. The restoration of Nationality to that party would be his greatest punishment.

The subject—however interesting—must be, for the present, abandoned, as the personal narrative of one of Mr. Yancey's many victims progresses.

The depot is reached—a ticket purchased—the car is entered—a rear seat occupied—a newspaper unfolded, and the persecuted, but guiltless citizen, apparently engrossed in its contents, keeps a continual scrutiny upon the persons entering the train.

Soon, the gathering feet of incomers, the musical voices of women, the harsher tones of men, all commingling in denunciation of the Union, are the sounds; Secession cockades, blue ribbons, inscribed with "*Resistere Lincolni est obedientia Deo*," Secession newspapers—these are the sights.

It was, of course, a relief to me, when the whistle blew, and, with its living freight, the locomotive started. The rattling of the cars soon drowned all voices save that of Memory.

Whither was I going? Should I successfully run the gauntlet of the State—of the South—what spot of earth could I call *home?* Where could I find a mother—brother—wife? Was I leaving my children, my home, forever? What eyes would weep at my departure, outside of my own immediate family? I had friends in Montgomery—*would they dare to defend the exile?* Would they, *without a single exception,* unite their voices in *reproach* of my oath-keeping actions? *or would some unquenchable spirit vindicate my name, cherish my memory, and await the day of my return?*

Such was the agony of my mind, that I almost resolved to return to the city and to invite my fate. It would have been a consolation, at that moment, if, devoting myself for the good of my fellow-citizens, I could have seen *one* soulful face catch my spirit as it ascended and beam it upon the crowd. If there was in the "City of the Great King," a soul attuned to the music of *true* South-

ern Rights, that soul knew not the fate of him who
was being so rapidly hurried away from the possibility of communication!

The cars stopped, as if merely to breathe, at a
station. The whistle blew, again we started in the
race (of life for some, of death for others), and
against the background of the forest which lined
the railroad, the following lines, from Moore,
seemed traced in one long telegram:

> "Far he fled—indignant fled,
> The pageant of his *country's* shame;
> While every tear her children shed
> Fell on his soul like drops of flame;
> And, as a lover hails the dawn
> Of a first smile, so welcomed he
> The sparkle of the first sword drawn—"
> For non-slave-owners' Liberty.

Alas! I have not yet seen, although I feel assured
I will some time see, that bright day-spring from
on high, when my country's flag will be the
cherished emblem of true Southern Rights!

The "nigger" can not long continue to be the all
absorbing idea! There must soon come a day when
the poor white men of this whole country will
come in for their rights.

So deeply has the administration party become
infatuated with one idea, that it hesitates at no
constitutional obstacle for the perpetration of its
single design. He who refuses to go to the *ultima
thule* of their desperation, and to advocate the in-
discriminate massacre of every loyal and disloyal

man, woman, and child of the whole South, is denominated a traitor; and, whatever may be his love of the flag of our common country, whatever his devotion to the name and the written principles of Washington, he is tormented with the suspicion of those whose unpatriotic aspiration is the subjugation to provincial vassalage of the Southern States, rather than their restoration to the Union.

Rome, the greatest military despotism ever known on earth, after conquering a nation, permitted it to become an honored part of her empire; but the Sumners and the Greeleys would be unsatisfied with any thing short of the perpetual vassalage (if they could only secure it) of every white person of the South. A loyal Southern man they hate and despise, unless he be also a greater friend to the black man than to his own downtrodden race. I speak solemnly and truly, when I profess my incompetency to discover any other future for the poor African than utter extermination, if the exasperating policy of the administration be persisted in.

The Southern people (and I know them well) will never permit the negroes to live among them, nominally their equals. They will make the South too hot for them, even if this war were to become a nigger-success, and the *protégées* of "Massa Greeley" would precipitate themselves like an avalanche upon Northern communities—naturally expecting fraternization and protection. These, everybody

knows, would be peremptorily denied them, and
thus they would become a race of vagabond ma-
rauders upon society, until mobocracy, that cruel
scourge of our country, would perpetuate itself
upon their destruction. If wholesome laws were
enacted for their regulation, their antecedents
would render it necessary to coerce them into an
involuntary obedience. Negro equality in the
North, as well as in the South, is an ethnological
impossibility. In saying this, I pay the same
compliment to the white men of the North as to
those of the South. Then would come the next
danger. Those who say the negro is superior to
the white man would, of necessity, join him in his
resistance of law, which his white friends would
call another kind of slavery. This would increase
the numbers of the negroes, but not their respectability, and scenes of horror would be the result,
which would render the brutalities of Southern
mobs no longer a "peculiar institution."

The proposition I made to the non-slaveholders
of Alabama, to confine, by law, the institution to
the cotton-fields, including, of course, the menial
offices of the household, and thus to rescue in the
South her mechanical pursuits from the hated
negro equality, while it would not have impaired
the intrinsic value of the property of the planters,
would have restored the "poor white trash," or
Southern "mudsills," to their long-lost Southern
Rights. This moderate course was one of the
causes of my banishment; and yet, were I to

suggest the same thing as the best policy of the United States Government, Radicals of all kinds would be ready to re-echo the old cry, "Crucify him!"

A proclamation by the President, rescinding the emancipation proclamation, and declaring all mechanical pursuits in the South to be sacred to the white man's free labor, at the same time confining the negroes in the Gulf States to the cultivation of cotton, sugar, and rice, and to menial household occupations; while, in the Border States, the mechanical pursuits being made equally free, the slaves shall be confined to the culture of tobacco and hemp, and to menial household employments, would create an awakening and a revulsion in the South which would restore the Union and save the administration.

The looms of manufacturing cities, domestic and foreign, would then be better than ever supplied, the planters would be reduced from their aristocratic pretensions, while not the least of its blessings would be the disinthrallment of the non-slave-owners, and, at the same time, the Union feeling of the South, so long held in check by the un-national, un-Caucasian, and un-constitutional course of the present infatuated administration.

After what seemed to be an age, I arrived at West Point, Georgia, whence I dispatched several letters to my brother, Marion C. Tharin, an engineer on the Charleston and Hamburgh railroad,

requesting him to bring, or send, some money to
me, as I was fleeing from *Mobocracy*, and had left,
in my haste, all save a few dollars.

Two days of suspense elapsed but no letter came.
Not only was my money ebbing away but my exposure was becoming imminent. To *earn* enough
to bear me away was my first thought. I am an
excellent penman, and my previous occupation of
teaching suggested something in that line as the
proper mode.

I saw some young ladies amusing themselves
on the green, in front of a long, low, white
building, which I judged to be the seminary.
I approached the building and inquired whether
it was an academy. I was politely informed,
by a young lady, that it was, and that its pre-
ceptress was then expected every moment—that,
if I would walk in and be seated, she would be informed, upon her arrival, that some one wished to
see her.

I entered the building and sat down in a kind of
parlor, where I had not long to wait before the intellectual face of the principal was presented at the
door. I rose respectfully, bowed profoundly, and
gave my name as Percy. Presenting the lady a
chair, we were soon immersed in a conversation,
which I am afraid detained her from more important, if not more interesting occupations.

After a pleasant and rather discursive conversation, I bowed myself out of the door, hat in hand,
with a vague presentiment that, unless relief came

soon, my failure to obtain a writing-class in that seminary would result in the most disastrous failure of my life.

Turning away I was proceeding toward the hotel, when a beautiful and intelligent face beamed a recognition upon me. For one brief moment I stood transfixed with incertitude, not knowing whether or not to speak. The last time I had seen that face was in Wetumpka, Alabama, where a frequent visitor at the house of Col. Saxon, a staunch Democrat of the Senator Fitzpatrick School, I was often thrown, before and since my marriage, into her company.

My hesitation was but momentary, however. For the first time in my life, I purposely turned away without speaking, from a lady of my acquaintance. Assuming the disguises of a stoop and a limp—neither of which is even remotely characteristic of my ordinary mode of procedure,— I hobbled away to the infinite surprise of Miss Charlotte Cherry, whose wonder-stricken countenance had not yet recovered its wonted expression, when I threw a retrospective glance over my shoulder.

The presence of an acquaintance in the Cotton State of Georgia, who knew me to be in West Point—if she had recognized me, and who, if she had not, would, woman-like, inform her friends in Alabama of the singular likeness between me and the gentleman who had visited the school—was a spur to my speed. The idea of remaining there was simply ridiculous. I might have applied, with impunity, to Miss Cherry for aid in procuring a situation in that academy ; but I would not involve her young life in the mesh of ruin in which King Cotton had involved me.

I had already suffered considerable anxiety, on account of the manner toward me of the railroad conductor from Montgomery, who rested each day a scrutinizing glance upon me, and, even, at last, asked me whether we had *met* before. There had been no previous acquaintance, and so I said. The man looked dissatisfied.

As soon as the return train started for Montgomery, I repaired to a teacher of the town, and laid my case before him. The good Christian heard me with tears, and invited me to dinner. There I was introduced to his family, who seemed very kind and sympathizing, although no word from the reverend gentleman described my predicament. The next northward train approaching, that true Christian gentleman went to the cars in company with his guest whom he had furnished with money to Chattanooga, Tennessee.

The reader will remember the great excitement of that time, the hatred of the cotton-planters to myself and my cause, and will not fail to see how important to the subsequent advantage of the non-slaveholding whites of the South was my escape — that is, the preservation of my testimony.

Arrived at Chattanooga, I registered my name

as R. Seymour (which is a part of my name); I
was about seeking my apartment when I was
"brought up all standing" at the door by the
familiar sound :

"Robert!"

I turned and beheld a fair complected youth
standing in the "passage."

REFUGEE. "You have the advantage, sir."

YOUTH. "Don't you remember me, Robert?"

REFUGEE. "I expect you make a mistake."

YOUTH. "Don't you remember Joseph Renard?"

REFUGEE. "You still have the advantage, sir."

YOUTH. "Did you not attend the Sunday-school
at St. John's Chapel, Charleston, many years
ago?"

REFUGEE. "I did."

YOUTH. "I was a pupil in the class taught by
your 'Uncle Edward.'"

We shook hands where we had conversed, full
in view and hearing of the book-keeper.

We took a walk together. Renard was an engineer on the Charleston and Chattanooga railroad. He expressed great sympathy for the
nephew of his former Sunday-school teacher, and
offered to procure me a free passage on the engine
to Nashville, the engineer being his friend. But,
repenting of his shallow impulse, the backslidden
Sunday-scholar left his "friend" to his fate. I
blush to admit that Renard is a non-slave-
owner.

No time was to be lost. The mob feeling had not yet culminated at Chattanooga; but to my eye—which was somewhat initiated, I may say—there were unmistakable signs in the political horizon. Again betaking myself to a clergyman I was aided on my way to Cincinnati.

Not feeling secure in the fidelity of Joseph Renard, I returned to the hotel, paid my bill, and started for the Lookout station on foot. As I was leaving the desk, the book-keeper said:

"Good morning, Mr. Tharin."

I suppose I owe that salutation and its accompanying wink to Joseph Renard, or else to him and my interlocutor together. The clerk looked surprised, when, with a calm smile, I returned his salutation.

I was completely exhausted when I arrived at the station. Some workmen were employed in bringing clay in cars, and emptying it along the road. Upon inquiry I found that some time would elapse before the train would pass. A gentlemanly person approached and invited me to supper. I accepted; but much did I wish afterward that I had declined. The language of the host consisted in an interminable panegyric on Jefferson Davis. Several times I was on the eve of betraying myself by an imprudent outburst. I took good care seemingly to agree with mine host, and evinced an intimate knowledge of the late movements of his pet, to the great delight of himself, and of his gaping family. But, even the most unpleasant circumstances have an end, and the whistle of the locomotive cheered the sinking heart of the impatient traveler.

Of my arrival at Cincinnati I have already treated in the Introduction to this personal narrative, to which the reader's attention is again invited for any personal testimonials he may have lost sight of. It will be remembered that in that chapter are set forth the proofs of my statements from the Cahawba *Gazette* (Dallas county, Ala.), as dictated by one of the mob, Robert Rives, and of the Maysville (Ky.) *Eagle*. In that chapter also are contained letters from Hon. Milton Sayler and Samuel Lowry, Esq., of Cincinnati, establishing my identity; from Judge Stallo and Rev. E. G. Robinson, of the Ninth-street Baptist Church, as to my habits and character; from William L. Yancey, dated 1859, in relation to our former law-partnership; from B. P. Baker, Esq., then of Cincinnati, now of New York, dated August 11, 1862, recommending me for loyalty, and alluding to the Union speech I had the honor to deliver to a large concourse of Cincinnatians; extracts from the Richmond (Ind.) *Palladium*, and the Centerville (Ind.) *True Republican*, in relation to my (involuntary) enlistment, as a private in the ranks, to the *credit* of which the Radicals of that little town are entitled; letters from Judge Perry and Benjamin Davis, Esq., to the Colonel of the 16th Indiana; the certificate of Captain Welsh, 7th Indiana, Com-

pany D., as to my actions at the Union victory at
Winchester, March 23, 1862, and a copy of my
letter to the London *Daily News*, entitled "Yancey and the Slave-trade," which was written in
reply to a note from Mr. Yancey to the London
Times, denying his advocacy of its renewal. My
reason for commencing this "Personal Narrative"
with the documents, alluded to above, was avow-
edly to prove my claim to the attention of my
fellow-citizens—to "pave the way" to a better
understanding of the autobiography which was to
follow.

Living all my life, up to the time of my exile,
in the sunny South, I claim to be better acquainted with her domestic condition than those who
have only seen the country through the eyes of
others ; and it may not be amiss for me to dwell
for a short time upon the exciting subject of this
gigantic rebellion, viewed in the general relations
of the North with the South, and *vice versâ*.

In the second chapter of this narrative, I have
given the concluding portion of my speech to the
citizens of Buyckville and vicinity, which affords
a veracious and unanswerable exposition of the
relative number and actual condition of the two
classes of the Cotton States, viz., the owners of
slaves, and the owners of no slaves. In that
speech, I protested against the tyranny of King
Cotton, and contrasted the *non-resident majority*
of the North with the *resident minority* of the
South, in a manner which was by no means flat-

tering to either the one or the other. It will be
remembered that I concluded that address with
this peroration :

" *That oath is registered in heaven!* I make no
light and foolish vows. That oath I intend to
keep *always;* and, if I lose all the tranquillity
and peace of mind I possess, that oath shall never,
at God's bar, reproach me, as it will yet reproach
many *other lawyers* and officers of Alabama with
perjury !" Also :

" In conclusion : what I have said, I have said
in strict accordance with ' *Southern Rights.*' If I
have the misfortune to differ with men of wealth
and influence, it shall, at least, never be said of
R. S. Tharin, that he is *afraid* to give a reason
for the faith that is in him !"

The reader will perceive, from this quotation,
that I feel as much bound " to support the Constitution and the Union" as I ever did, and that I
am *still* unpledged to any other course !

From the manner in which I have already defended the Constitution and the Union in the
South, it is easy to see whether a radical course
can consistently be expected of me now, or at any
future time, in the North.

I have now completed a part of the undertaking
I have assumed; and, perhaps, here I should
pause, as at the last milestone on a rough and
perilous road, but I *can not.* The same *oath,*

which, in the sight of God and man, I registered
in the sweet spring of 1859, at Rockford court-
house, Coosa county, Alabama, still animates my
conscience, and demands my activity.

In the foregoing pages, I have attempted to de-
pict the atrocities of that Reign of Terror which
culminated in deeds of license and of blood, which
violated the sanctity of law, which disregarded
the awful sanction of solemn oaths, which ravened
at the throats of Justice, Mercy, and the Constitution. I have "nothing extenuated, nor set down
aught in malice;" but, were I to stop here, I would
be unworthy the martyrdom I have suffered for
the liberty of speech—that birthright of Americans *everywhere;* unworthy of my whig ancestry
of 1776, who fought to insure me the rights of
Magna Charta under the Constitution of the
United States! Action and Reaction being "equal
and in opposite directions," the scenes which filled
the South with horror and disgrace, have been,
alas! re-enacted in the North, and, long after a
shadow of excuse seems, even to the most bigoted
Radical, to exist for the most unconstitutional pro-
cedures, *American citizens* are, upon the slightest
pretences, hauled before military satraps, and incarcerated in loathsome dungeons, hopeless of release, and beyond the benign reach of the Constitution itself.

It is the duty of every lawyer who has taken the
lawyer's oath, to remonstrate *openly* and at the

risk of life, if need be, against these unjustifiable and unconstitutional usurpations!

Here, in the Northern States—here, in the national capital—where armed rebellion has left no footprint upon the soil, the people should be left to discuss, in primary assemblages, their interests as a people. The people of the Northern not less than of the Southern States, are denied that right by armed minorities, who madly persist in making *a political bias the test of loyalty.* The man who submits to such an outrage, North or South, is a *slave.* The voice of Washington has long since been drowned in the clamor of demagogues and the roar of artillery. The 22d of February, 1863, which has scarcely left the present, bears to the record of the past only reproaches for our slavishness and demands on our thoughtful and most candid consideration. Is the Union, bequeathed to us by the Father of our country, to be lost in the maëlstrom of war, because no man dare incur the fearful risk of proposing a plan of reconstruction? Are American citizens, North and South, the abject slaves of their respective tyrannies? *Why* do they not restore the democratic party to its *nationality,* and reconstruct the Union upon the ruins of sectionalism? Would any humble citizen of either section be the worse off because of the re-establishment of law? Are we so much attached to the names of our corrupters as to desire the perpetuity of their sanguinary rule? Has martial law done so much for the sections that both

20

prefer it to the Union of our forefathers? Does a
military despotism in either section delight the
victims of an artificial crisis—on the despotic and
un-American basis of "military necessity?" Have
the people of the "loyal North" forgotten the principle adopted by an almost unanimous Congress
for the prosecution of this war? What were their
words?

"That this war is not waged on their part in any
spirit of oppression, or for any purpose of over-
throwing or interfering with the rights and established institutions of the States, but to defend and
maintain the supremacy of the Constitution, and
to *preserve* the Union with all the dignity, equality,
and rights of the several *States* unimpaired, and
that, as soon as these objects are accomplished,
the war ought to cease."

The duty of a State in rebellion is to return to
the Union—but radicals insinuate that, having
seceded, they have degenerated into territories
and must become subject to the *will* of the minority ·who now hold the archives of the National
Government. The wildest theories and most crazy
theorists have perforated the brain of the Cabinet,
and CHASE each other, like maggots, around the
raw head and bloody bones of the Presidential
edict. The President, despairing of the support
of the conservative people of the country in car-
rying out his own personal notions, has appealed
in "the proclamation" to the *negroes*, whose antecedents have proved them no warrior race, who,

as a people, cannot read his decree, and whose masters have coerced not only them, but, also, the white Unionists who *once* doubted the designs of the Northern radicals.

In the chapter of this work, styled SCENE THE FIFTH, I have shown that the non-slave-owners of the South are doomed to a partial negro-equality through the *abuse*, by the planters, of the institution of Slavery, which, like *all* other institutions, is subject to abuse, and that the only shadow of superiority left them by the Rebel leaders is the nominal and actual slavery of the inferior race.

There was—may it soon return!—a time when the division between the Disunionists and Unionists of the South constituted the greatest obstacle in the path of the Rebellion, although covered up by the plastic hand of Deception. Skillfully and patriotically addressed, the old Union feeling of the South, which for almost half a century had stood the test of the united efforts of the Aristocrats, would have risen in overwhelming force to crush out rebellion in their midst; but the Administration has seen fit to address the *negroes* on a subject beyond their comprehension (and their true interests, by the by), and thus has disgusted and alienated the conservatism of the white people of the South, who can only be won back to their Unionism by the wise and prudent action of the Conservatives of the North.

The following extract from "Jeff. Davis's Message," while it confirms the historical portion of the above argument, at the same time, enforces the conclusion by admitting the premises:

"In its political aspects this measure possesses great significance, and to it, in this light, I invite your attention. It affords to our whole people the complete and crowning *proof** of the true nature of the designs of the party which elevated to power the present occupant of the Presidential Chair at Washington, and which sought to conceal its purpose by every variety of artful device, and by the perfidious use of the most solemn and repeated pledges on every possible occasion. . . . . . The people of the Confederacy, then, can not fail to receive this proclamation as the *fullest vindication of their own sagacity in foreseeing* the uses to which the dominant party in the United States intended from the beginning to apply their power ;. nor can they cease to remember with devout thankfulness that it is to their own vigilance in resisting the first stealthy progress of approaching despotism that they owe their escape from consequences *now apparent to the most skeptical.*†

"It is, also, in effect, an intimation to the people of the North that they must prepare to submit to a separation, now become inevitable ;‡ for that people are too acute not to understand that a resto-

---

* Of what the planters most eagerly desire of all things.

† *Now* apparent to those who were for the Union while they doubted it—he means.

‡ Because of the blind folly of the Administration in antagonizing every element of the South.

ration of the Union has been rendered forever impossible *by the adoption* of a measure which, from its nature, *neither admits of retraction* nor can coexist with them.*

" Humanity shudders at the appalling atrocities which are being daily multiplied under the sanction of those who have claimed *temporary*† possession of the power in the United States, and who are fast making its once fair name a by-word of reproach among civilized men. Not even the natural indignation inspired by this conduct should make us, however, so unjust as to attribute to the whole mass of the people, who are subjected to the despotism that now reigns with unbridled license in the city of Washington, a willing acquiescence in the conduct of the war. *There must necessarily exist among our enemies, very many, perhaps a majority, whose humanity recoils from all participation in such atrocities, but who can not be held wholly guiltless, while permitting their continuance without an effort at repression.*" A bid to Northern *Secessionists.*

The last sentence of the above message of the

---

* You see *he* does not desire its retraction, having labored to produce it—but the Conservatives will yet repeal it in time to save the Union. Foreign mediation we do not want—will not permit—but the mediation of the common sense of the American masses—that we *will* have!

† This word is used to confound the counsels of the Unionists of the South, who are willing to return under certain circumstances, and is used as a dissuasive argument.

despot of the South, is a two-edged sword which
militates against his own desires as well as against
the desires of the despot of the North. *Both* have
become obnoxious to the majority in both sections,
and both will perish in the indignation which now
agitates the American blood of the "very many
(in *both* sections) *perhaps* majorities, whose humanity recoils from all participation in such atrocities, *but who can not be held wholly guiltless while
permitting their continuance (in either section)
without an effort at repression.*"

Let Jeff. Davis remember that there are Conservatives *South* as well as North, and in the name
of both I proclaim that "the Union must and shall
be preserved," forcibly if we must—peaceably if
we can!

The proclamation of the President is impolitic
as a "war measure," because, in theory, it removes
from the poor conscript of the South the only
proof of his superiority to the black slave, and
thus arms him with a vengeance against the President, which, with all his vaporing, he never felt
before.   It affords an excuse, also, for the conscription of the black into the armies of Secession
to meet the "black soldiers" of the President, and
tends to the ultimate extirpation of the negro race
by a "military necessity."   Such is the *philan-
thropy* of the measure!

The *duty* of this Government is to *weaken* the
Rebels by its good policy, while it overwhelms their
armies by its power.   If it fails to conquer them

by arms and good policy combined, it must be
because of their numbers, or of their intrenchments, or of their strategy, or of their unity, or
of some or all of these combined. If any act of
the Government, or of him who dictatorially constitutes himself the Government, be calculated,
proprio vigore, to increase the numbers or the
unity of the Rebels, to strengthen their intrenchments, to improve their strategy, or to produce
some or all of these bad results, then is that act
impolitic and *unmilitary*.

Now I have proved, and have made Jeff. Davis
himself an unwilling witness, that the Emancipation Proclamation is the very best means of har-
monizing the otherwise conflicting interests of the
Rebels, by taking away from the non-slave-owner
of the South the only proof he has of his political
superiority to the slave-owner's black serf, and his
only argument against the planter. Therefore, I
have proved from a Southern point of view, that
the proclamation is impolitic and *unmilitary*.

From a Northern point of view, the "imperial
policy" of the President is very poor policy, because it obviously produces the most lamentable
results upon the people and the soldiery. Therefore, again I say it is impolitic and *unmilitary*.

But does not the President claim the right of
issuing his imperial edict by virtue of a "military
necessity?"

How can that be a *military necessity* which is
itself *un*military?

During the Presidential contest, which resulted in the lamentable elevation of—Jeff. Davis to the first office in the so-called Southern Confederacy, it was the favorite argument of the precipitators in the Cotton States, that negro equality was the intention of the Republican party.* It seems to me I can see William L. Yancey addressing the people of some Southern community in these words:

"Did we not tell you so? Compare our predictions with the event, and you behold the perfect proof of our declarations!"

Thus, the shallow policy of the Administration is calculated to produce the result of confirming predictions upon which the rebellion was founded!

This work was written—except a few notes and some alterations necessitated by the last act of the Radicals—long before September 22d, 1862, and, therefore, is much more calm in its strictly narrative parts than in these concluding remarks, which are written in alarm lest the last rail split by "Old Abe" be the Union, for which I risked my *life* in the South, and for which I risk my *liberty* in the North! But the "imperial policy," so-called, of the radical cabinet is the very policy most desired by the chiefs of the Rebellion, for, while it shocks the common sense of the country, even of Abolitionists, if they have any, and thus divides the "loyal North," it "fires the Southern

---

* See p. 44, for extract of Speech of Hon. Jabez L. M. Curry, at Wetumpka, Alabama.

heart" more universally than did the mere election of him who "presides over *our* destinies," but is blind to *his own !*

There is, however, one aspect of this "imperial policy," which is not calculated to soothe a spirit, who has borne open testimony in the North* and in the South† to his heart-rending conviction that *England* is the fomenter of our troubles, and that it is *her* imperial policy to divide and conquer this Union, even as the two Grecian States of Athens and Sparta were divided and conquered by the machinations of Philip of Macedon. *Our* Philip of Macedon sits (in petticoats) upon the English throne. Hob-nobbing with the heads of rebellion, over which she suspended glittering coronets, and over one a vice-royal crown, she promised them her support, and after she found them engaged as "belligerents," she professed—through the London *Times*—her willingness to "recognize" them, because the *North* was upholding slavery by adhering to the Constitution of the country. Thus, by skillfully manipulating her puppet vicegerents of the North, she has inaugurated her "imperial policy" through Mr. Chase, and scarcely waits for the ink of the (British) proclamation of the President to dry, before she publishes, through the London *Times*, that slavery is to be justified on Scriptural grounds. During all this time, by her "proclamation" of neutrality, she puts in practice

* See Introduction, p. 18. † See p. 47.

the "masterly inactivity," which the Roman historian Tacitus unconsciously suggested to Mr.
Calhoun, who—plagiarist as he was—appropriated
the credit due to another man.

It is the old story. "History is ever re-enacting
itself." Sparta was the enemy of Athens, even as
the Rebels of the South are the enemies of the
North, and the Macedonian monarch, seizing upon
domestic feuds, first aggravated, then dismembered
Greece, which soon fell a victim to the "imperial
policy" of a weaker but more insidious foe.

The three classes of society in Sparta, or *Ancient
Secessia*, were exactly similar to the three classes
of society in Modern Secessia. If the first had her
Homoii,* or *Superiors*, who alone held office, the
second has her First Families, or Planters, who
illegally monopolize the official honors, emoluments, and influence of the South ;† if the first had
her Hypomeiones,‡ or Inferiors, who were allowed
to vote but not hold office, *by* law, the second has
her "poor white trash," who are excluded from
office *against* law ;† if the first had her Helots,§ or
Slaves, who held neither office nor vote, which, as
they were white men, was wrong, the second has
her Africans, or Slaves, who, being black, *right-
fully* hold neither vote nor office.

Thus you perceive that Philip of Macedon naturally sought, as allies, the Homoii or Superiors of
Sparta, who, growing tired of Grecian Union,

---

* Ὁμοιι.   † See p. 70, *Ante*.   ‡ Ὑπομειονες.   § Ἱλοτες.

manifested the spirit of " Oh ! that we had one of the royal family (of Macedon) to rule over us !" *

Ancient Secessia had by law *two* kings.

Modern Secessia *has* " King Cotton," and longs for a British Prince.

Thus the parallel is complete, and as Greece fell from disunion, before the Macedonian phalanx, so we will fall, if we remain dismembered—*both* sections will fall—before European diplomacy.†

It becomes the war-ridden *people* of both sections, therefore, to reconstruct the Union, and to present to foreign nations, once and forever, a front unbroken and one.

Washington was *right* when he said, " The Union is the palladium of your *safety.*" Nor was he wrong when he wrote :

---

* London *Times* Russell.

† The name of NAPOLEON is prophetic of *his* purpose. By dropping letter by letter from the Greek name, Ναπωλεον, we have a Greek sentence complete, which signifies—Napoleon being a lion, is going forth *from* a lion, the destruction of cities.

We all know that he took refuge, for a time, in England, the emblem of which is a Lion ; when he went to France and became emperor, he, therefore, went from a lion, and proved himself a lion ; and now he roars at the cannon's mouth at Puebla (next door to the United and Confederate States), that he has come to devour American cities. For the information of the curious I will here state that the Greek sentence, foreshadowing all this, runs thus : Ναπολεων, απολεον, πολεων, ολεων, λεων, εων, ων.

Let my countrymen then beware of *mediation* from Napoleon—and of Jewett, whose name is capable of a damaging and ignoble construction.

"There can be no greater error than to expect, or calculate upon, real favors from nation to nation. It is an illusion which experience must cure, *which a just pride ought to discard.*" *

But, in these days of tumult, the radical howlings, North *and* South, have drowned the voice of the Father of his Country. In vain he pleads with his disobedient children. The Radicals of the South and of the North have alike invited England to interfere in our troubles, the one by bidding for recognition, and the other by bidding against it. It is treason to the whole *people* to bid for the subjugation of any part of them.

Meanwhile, the Lion of England steals through the forest, scenting his prey. His hot breath is almost on our faces, his mane is gradually bristling

---

* "FAREWELL ADDRESS"—*all* of which seems at this time more like the inspiration of a prophet than the production of a mere statesman. The reader can not too often peruse Washington's Farewell Address. For instance, what can be more sublime than the following tearful plea: "In offering to you, my countrymen, these counsels of an old and affectionate friend, I dare not hope they will make the strong and lasting impression I could wish; *that they will control the usual current of the passions, or prevent our nation from running the course which has hitherto marked the destiny of nations;* but if I may even flatter myself that they may be productive of some partial benefit, *some occasional good;* that they may now and then recur *to moderate the fury of party spirit, to warn against the mischiefs of foreign intrigues, to guard against the impostures of pretended patriotism;* THIS HOPE will be a full recompense for the solicitude for your welfare by which they have been dictated." Shall that hope be disregarded?

with anticipated vengeance, his roar will soon shake the atmosphere—will my countrymen, North and South, permit all the blessings achieved by the sword of our Washington, to be lost through neglect of his farewell advice?

With the above pregnant question, I conclude this work, which will soon be followed by another, entitled "Results of my Southern and Northern Experience," which will be presented under the form of three historical parallels, *with a proposed plan of reconstruction.*

Hoping soon to meet the reader again, I now bid him a temporary adieu, and as I stand, *pour prendre congé,* with the door-knob in my left hand, with my right I wave him an   *Au revoir!*

LETTER FROM THE AUTHOR TO HIS MOTHER.

NEW YORK, February 15th, 1863.

MY DEAR MOTHER:

This month, two long and dreary years ago, I was dragged from your arms by an infuriated mob of demons, and driven a fugitive from my adopted State of Alabama.

Since that hour, the war, which to foretell and endeavor to prevent was my only crime, has deluged your native Virginia in blood, and double-locked the portals of intelligence, at which I have knocked and waited in vain for news of you and my only brother.

During that fearful time, while Liberty has bidden adieu to the *whole country*, and arbitrary arrests have filled the bastiles of the South and of the North with victims of a duplicate despotism, I have many times essayed to write to you and brother Marion; but no means of transportation for letters has been offered, because Mr. Lincoln was afraid I would say something revealing the Union element of the North, which is not tainted with Abolitionism, and Mr. Davis was afraid I would say something appealing to the Union element of the South, which is untainted with Secessionism.

The mutual jealousy of these two satraps of each other, and of every thinking mind and speaking tongue and pen in the Republic, would be amusing, dear mother, if it were not so dreadful in its results. Radicalism, or Sectionalism, South and North, delighting in extremes and rioting in anarchy, has planted the dagger into our bleeding hearts, and then commands the mother and her persecuted son to hold no intercourse in a country once free to the feet and the lips of millions of now trampled serfs.

Having failed so often in getting news of you or to you by the ordinary modes of communication, I include this letter in my book, hoping that some good soul will convey the whole work to your hand and thus soothe your sorrows by this fleeting glimpse of your exiled son.

I am agonized with the unwelcome but often

recurring thought that, perhaps, we are never more to see each other in the flesh. The fearful vision of your decease is even now rending asunder the chords of my heart. The shroud and the coffin may, ere this, have intervened their spectral folds, the spring verdure may be even now waving above a new-made grave, in which reposes the unwaking eyes of my aged mother! while I am not permitted by the fiends of mobocracy to drop a tear, or to plant a rose upon her last resting-place.

These thoughts have preyed upon my mind and upon my health. In addition to these reflections, my wife and children are in very poor health, and the former mourns, like me, over absent relations, whom she may never more behold. Her old mother, like you, is bereaved of a child by the atrocious usurpations of King Cotton and Emperor Davis. Like you, she has a son forced, by circumstances beyond his control, into the armies of Southern Despotism. Thus I carry a triple burden, and can only see in a peaceful reconstruction of the National Democratic Party on a constitutional basis, and a reconstruction of the old, or a more liberal, Union, by means of the united action of Unionists South and North, any hope of ever seeing again my kith and kin, any hope of civilization, or of what our Litany prays every Sabbath, that God will give to *all* nations—" unity, peace, and concord."

If this letter ever reaches you, dear mother (and I sometimes indulge the fond hope that it will find

its way by some benevolent hand to your possession), let it assure you, a thousand times, of my
safety, my affection, and my uncorrupted Unionism and honor. I am still as true to my oath, as
when I resisted arbitrary arrests in the Cotton
State of Alabama. *I counsel all patriots everywhere to resist them*, and to unite on Washington's
Farewell Address, Magna Charta, the bills of
rights of the several States, and the Constitutional
guarantees of the whole nation, and *conserve* the
interests of Religion, Liberty, Law, Commerce,
and Common Sense, ere the foreign powers, seeing our divisions to be incurable, pounce down
upon the sheepfold, and raven like wolves at the
throats of our blood-bought rights and national
glories.

You see how impossible it is for me to write
without advocating the Union before I stop. For
this I was arbitrarily arrested in Alabama, and
may be again despotically arrested in the North ;
but " sink or swim, live or die, survive or perish,
I give my hand and my heart" to the Union and
to the liberties of its oppressed citizens.

There are two parties in this country who desire
the destruction of the Union, viz. : the Abolitionists and Secessionists. To neither of these do I
belong. " When I forget thee, O Jerusalem !
may my tongue cleave to the roof of my mouth !"

Remember me affectionately to all my kinsfolk
and acquaintances. *God* made men to differ, *Sa-
tan* converts differences, which are in themselves

good gifts for the enlargement of knowledge, into hatred and war. I do not hate but love my friends who differ rationally from me. If, under the madness of the hour, any old friend turn against me on account of opinion, I suppose I must wait for the cooling of the nation in the tears of repentance before I can win him back.

To my beloved brother convey my unwavering love. Please, mother, plant upon dear father's grave a rose for me. I will yet press his sacred dust with pilgrim feet, when war shall cease and a nation's wounds are closing up.

God bless you. Good-by.

Your affectionate son,
ROBERT.

21*